ZEN AND THE ART OF SONGWRITING

By Dr. Coy Hurd

Cover image courtesy of *Poinsett County Democrat Tribune* and Mark Randall.

© 2024 by Coy Hurd

All rights reserved. No part of this publication may be reproduced or transmitted in any form, by any means, electronic or mechanical, including photocopy recording or any informational storage and retrieval system now known or to be invented or any which are unknown at this time, without permission in writing from the publisher, except by a reviewer who wishes to quote brief passages in connection to a review written for inclusion in a magazine, newspaper, or broadcast.

Library of Congress Cataloging of Publication Data is available.

ISBN 979-8-218-57279-2

Everywhere I go, the peoples are always asking me,
"Manchild, how come you always be singing them sad, sad songs?"
I just tell them,
"Them sad, sad songs is all that I know."

Manchild Razor
From somewhere in the Delta

Courtesy *KAIT*

PROLOGUE: THE MAXIE

I like to watch the Turner Channel and all those great old movies they show, especially the noir movies. I feel comfortable when I watch one of those old flicks, like saying hello to a long-lost friend. It's a similar feeling to hearing the Andy Griffith theme song playing in the next room. There are a few movies that have been lodged in my psyche for one reason or another, then I see them as an adult. Somehow there is a strong sense of closure there. For a long run of years, I saw most every movie that was made in Hollywood, I saw each of them several times. That's why I like the old black and whites so much now.

My parents owned the movie theater in the small town where I was raised. My father, John, was an entrepreneur. He farmed and did other things too. One of these projects was the Maxie Theater. I was born in 1947 and the Maxie was built that same year.

Some of my first recollections revolve around the Maxie. My parents took me along as they worked at starting their business. We would go each afternoon. There was a good deal of time before any paying customers showed. Meanwhile, John would start a music tape on an old Wollensak reel-to-reel recorder. This was broadcast into the auditorium through huge metal-horn speakers. The sound of this rudimentary set was fantastic. Of course, this same tape played night after night. It wasn't long before I had heard these songs dozens of times, over and over.

John's tape had some great songs on it. There were Patsy Cline hits like *Walkin' After Midnight.* Webb Pierce had several songs on the mix, including *There Stands the Glass* and *Wondering.* All the hits were on that tape. Listening to these songs was how I got interested in music at a very young age. Even today some of my favorites are tunes that I heard on John's tape.

The first time I saw a live performance was at the C&R Club, a roadhouse just outside of town on Highway 63. I was eight years old. The C&R Club was plugged into the Memphis Musician's Union and booked some of the best rockabilly acts from Sun Records. The Colonel wouldn't book Elvis at the C&R because of its rough reputation. People had been shot and stabbed in the parking lot.

My neighborhood buds were nephews of the manager of C&R, and we would sneak in through the night club's back door, on through the kitchen, behind the bar. I could pull myself up and peek over to see the goings-on. I have a vivid memory of Billy Lee Riley and the Little Green Men as they belted out their latest hits, *Flying Saucer Rock 'n' Roll* and *Red Hot.*

SLIM RHODES

Slim was from Memphis and had a TV show on Chanel Five. He would have his entire extended family up on the stage playing music. At times there were three generations on the stage at once. Slim always did a great job, and he really did pique my interest. I wanted to be in a band too. Through his family band, he launched musical careers spanning generations, and they are still going strong today in Branson.

Every three months or so, Mr. Hendrix would engage the Slim Rhodes Show for a performance designed to stir up enthusiasm for the Liberty Cash. It worked. For a stage, a flatbed was parked in the parking lot between the Liberty Cash and the Maxie. Come show time, the parking lot was full of folks anxious to hear Slim.

I was influenced by Slim to start a long term, lifetime devotion to performing music on the stage.

MY FIRST JOB

I've always had a great deal of luck as far as jobs are concerned. My first real job was at the Liberty Cash Grocery Store on Highway 63. This grocery store was literally just a few steps from my home. As a small child, I liked to come over to the store for an ice cream treat. Once I climbed the refrigerated ice cream box and stretched too far. I fell into the freezer. Mr.

Hendrix walked over and grabbed the waist of my jeans to pull me out. When I was a youngster, I had total run of the grocery store. My modis was to enter the store by way of the backdoor. That door opened onto a large space used mostly for storage.

Every Christmas season, Mr. Hendrix would invite Santa Claus to drop by to meet and visit the children. I was very excited to get to see him, I couldn't control my enthusiasm. At the appointed time, I ran out of our backdoor and in the backdoor of the Liberty Cash. There stood Santa naked and about to don the red suit. Me and Santa were both speechless. I ran on through the room and into the front of the store. A few days later I told the story to my younger cousin, Jimmy, about what I had witnessed. I was sternly rebuked by Jimmy's parents for spreading falsehoods about Saint Nick. I liked the people there and enjoyed working for Mr. Hendrix. My main duty in the store was to sack groceries and carry them to the customer's waiting car. But at other times I did things like work in the meat market and then in the produce. Every Friday night, we would mop and wax the sizeable store. Soon I was saving for a car and that would change everything.

WHITE SHOES BAND

My first experience of being in a music combo was in third grade. One of my classmates was Barry. He was a leader for the others and had us marching in step around the playground. Barry heard about a talent contest to be held in a few days at school. He resolved to form a band and win the prize (a tin goblet). Barry immediately started putting his band together and called a practice for Saturday.

Saturday came and we showed up at Barry's. I really didn't know what to expect because none of us five had an instrument or knew anything at all about playing music. We only knew we liked rock 'n' roll and wanted to have a band. Our practice consisted of sitting around in Barry's bedroom listening to a record of Jerry Lee Lewis singing *Great Balls of Fire* a couple dozen times or more. We were learning by osmosis.

After that we got around to more important issues: what would our stage uniform be, as we all had to dress alike on stage. Someone suggested we all wear white shoes. These white shoes were a particular item of the day, not the white gym shoes we wear today, but suede saddle oxfords with brown soles that created a very cool look. Berry and one of the others already had such shoes. Sorry to say, I only had one pair of shoes, the high-top kind of basketball shoes, black. But no, Barry insisted; the band would be The White Shoes Band. So, I went to my mother and explained. I thought that when she saw how important these shoes were to my future success, how could she say no? As you might imagine, I did not get very far with her. "No, no white shoes for you, and don't bring it up again." I reported back to my comrades and was immediately fired from the band.

BILLY LEE RYLEY

Sonny and David and myself, we played a lot of sports in the neighborhood. Mostly football. They did a good job considering what they had to work with (me). I was ten years old and they were a couple of years older. We also spent a good deal of time listening to Sonny's forty-five record player. He had a lot of rockabilly songs because he got all the promotional records sent to Buddy, his uncle and manager of the C&R. Our favorite records which we played so much were *Who Do You Love* by Ronnie Hawkins and *Flyin' Saucer Rock 'n' Roll* by Billy Lee

Ryley and the Little Green Men. If you haven't checked Ryley out, look him up on YouTube. One morning Sonny told me that Buddy would sneak us in to see the show if we would act right. Wonderful. It was what we wanted more than anything.

Three days passed, and finally, here comes the big Saturday and the short trip of two miles to the C&R. We were glad to hear that Ronnie Hawkins was playing the first set. Ronnie's band at the time was the group of men destined to become The Band (minus Ronnie). Buddy had told Sonny that we could come around to the dressing room and actually meet the band, The Little Green Men. We walked around the bar to the changing rooms to the east. Buddy knocked on the door and we entered. Standing there smoking cigars were Jerry Lee Lewis and Rowland Janes. What a thrill! Soon, someone came to the room and announced that Ronnie was playing his last song, to get ready.

The club was totally packed that night and went crazy when Ryley cranked up. In quick fashion he played through his hits, *Flying Saucer Rock 'n' Roll*, *Red Hot* and *Pearlie Lee*. To say that he was well received would be an understatement.

Billy Lee Ryley went on to record several more records on the Sun label, but never could seem to get another hit. Word had it that Sam Phillips and Billy Lee had a feud and he never would spend any money to promote Billy Lee's efforts.

During the next several years, Billy Lee was pretty much off the grid. He was rediscovered by Bob Dylan in the mid-seventies. Dylan claimed to be a devoted fan since 1955, but then Ryley went back into semi-obscurity.

Forty years would pass before I would see Billy again. I was reading a U of A newsletter when I saw an article about an upcoming address by Billy Lee to take place in Giffels Auditorium a few days later. What a metamorphism -- rockabilly to university lecturer.

I showed up a bit early in the evening. Someone was standing just outside the door smoking. I got closer and could see it was Ronnie Hawkins, come to see his good friend make a speech. I said, "Hey Uncle Ronnie, wanna jam?" Ronnie looked at me and said, "No, I don't wanna jam. If I play music, I wanna get paid!"

Billy Lee did well that night talking about the good ole days of Sun Records. He got around to the part where the floor opened for questions from the audience. Someone asked about the feud with Sam Phillips. Billy collected his thoughts and said, "The last time I spoke to Sam Philips he was working with Elvis on a voice-over. They were using a Wollensak half-track recorder. I was drinking bourbon from a gallon jug. Sam made some wise-assed remark and so I turned that bottle upside-down on the Wollensak, tapes and all. That's the last time I ever saw Sam or Elvis."

DAN

I have a couple of friends that I have known for a long time, Dan and Eddie. Dan is the person that started me performing songs in public. He has been my good friend since 1956 when we were in the same fourth grade class. In high school, Dan's family moved to another town not so far away. I would go see him often; ride the bus or, later on, drive.

In the fourth grade, Dan was very much into pop songs, kind of how things are today. One song we liked was *Come Softly to Me* by the Fleetwoods. Dan asked me "Do you want to pantomime that song in front of the class?" I responded that sure, I could do that. We recruited three girls that we liked and scheduled a practice. At this practice, it became evident to me where this project was headed, but I guess I hoped for the best.

We had worked it all out with our teacher, Ms. Baker. She allowed us to stay inside during recess to rehearse. When the class returned, Ms. Baker told them that we had a real treat in store then called the group to the front. I started getting cold feet. I told Ms. Baker that I had changed my mind, I did not want to do the pantomime after all. Ms. Baker said to me, "No, no, you stayed in at recess and now you have to do the song."

We approached the front of the room with trepidation. Dan put on the 45 record and adjusted the needle. We indeed started to pantomime the song. I was very nervous about the whole thing, even after we put in some fancy dance steps we had invented. In the end we all survived unscathed that day.

Recently, I looked it up on Facebook: *Come Softly to Me* by the Fleetwoods. It sent a chill down my spine when I played it. I asked Dan if he wanted to write a song by email. He said sure. Well, did he have any ideas? He told me he wanted to write a song about the American heart. He wanted to write a song that they would play in the White House on the 4th of July. I got the picture.

EDDIE

I got to know Eddie through Dan. They were friends and were in bands together too, under the name of The Mystics. I saw Eddie's band on KAIT-TV. Dan called me and told me to come up and play for their prom. We had a great time.

I asked Eddie too; did he want to write a song by email and did he have any ideas? Yes, he did. He wanted to write a song about George Jones. Wonderful! Looking back, it's one of the best songs of the set: *Snownin' in May*.

Eddie and Bobby Bare

In the fall of 1964, Eddie's band, The Mystics, won the talent contest at the Sharp County Fair. There was nothing for the winners but blue ribbons, which each of them probably threw in the trash. It was Eddie's senior year in high school and his band, The Four Shadows, had come into its own. They were a pretty fair group of musicians and, while they did not have a great repertoire of songs, they played those they knew very well. The Mystics had broken up as one was drafted and another got married, and so this new group was Eddie's main interest in life now.

He was in the local barber shop one day after school when the county extension agent came in for a haircut. The agent told Eddie that he had been trying to get in touch with him for a couple weeks. He said that since The Mystics had won the county talent contest, The Four Shadows were invited to participate in a state-wide talent show and concert at Barton Coliseum in Little Rock. He gave Eddie a little flyer about it, which indicated that it was called Teen Jamboree '65 and was sponsored by the American Milk Producers Association or some similar milk producer's organization. In fact, there were several of these Teen Jamborees scheduled across the country.

The event featured a day-long talent contest and a musical concert to top the event off that Saturday night. The featured entertainers were Bobby Bare and Johnny Tillotson. Both were extremely popular pop artists during the early and mid '60s.

"Of course we will go," he told the extension agent and immediately went to look up his buddies and tell them the good news. They had matching red blazers to wear, so they would look good; and, as they were allocated only a small amount of time on the contest, their three great instrumental songs would knock the judges out: *Apache*, *Walk Don't Run* and *Sleepwalk*. The only problem was that their drummer did not have a great set of drums and his cymbals were especially lacking. Of course, they did not have the money to go out and purchase a good set of Zildjians, even used ones. But Eddie came up with a solution.

There was an old-time attorney in Hardy by the name of Carmack Sullivan, who was semi-wealthy and eccentric. He often drank profusely and maintained an office on Main Street in Hardy, in a large building which he owned. He was a very well-educated man and came from one of the first families to settle in the Hardy area. Carmack, as everyone called him, loved to play the trumpet, and had played in a band sometime back in his younger days in the 1930s. Many a night, after the movie theater in Hardy closed for the evening, old Carmack would come down the stairs of his building, drunk, in a nightgown or pjs blowing his trumpet. It was a sight to see. When he was sober, he was known as one of the best attorneys in Arkansas. He was close friends with Eddie's mom and dad, who had grown up in the area with him. Often, he would come to their house at night, half tooted; and Eddie's dad would take him home. So, Eddie knew the man well. Carmack liked to party a lot and had a lady friend that loved to party just as much. They both were managing the Woodland Hills Land

Development Company, which was just east of the Hardy city limits. It became a smaller model of Cherokee Village, which had been opened by John Cooper some years earlier.

Carmack was very nostalgic and always wanted to go back to his younger days. So, he decided to organize a jazz and blues band based on the one he had played in as a young man. During this time, there were a lot of new people moving into the Hardy area, many of which were working in lot sales at the four land developments that were thriving in the area: Cherokee Village, Hidden Valley, Woodland Hills and Ozark Acres. Some of the new guys were accomplished musicians and Carmack began to recruit a few of them to form his band. The only problem was that they had no one to play drums. So, sometimes they would borrow The Four Shadows' drummer for an engagement; but it did not work out very well because the drummer had little interest or talent for jazz-type music. To solve this problem, Carmack went out and bought his lady friend an expensive set of Slingerland drums, fully set with all available Zildjian cymbals. There. The problem was solved… or was it?

Well, Carmack's lady friend, Ms. T as she was called, had absolutely no rhythm or musical talent; nor did she have any patience or desire to learn. Therefore, this fine and expensive set of drums sat in the den of his house collecting dust.

Keep in mind, The Four Shadows were four 17-year-old kids who knew very little about the world outside and most of them had been no further from home than Memphis or Little Rock on one or two occasions. Eddie came up with the idea of talking to Carmack and telling him about the opportunity and their dilemma of having no drums fit to play for such an event. Thinking Carmack would be proud for some local kids to get such an opportunity, Eddie felt there was a good chance he would agree to let them use his Slingerlands for this event. So, one afternoon after school they went to his office to discuss the plan with him and Ms. T. At first, she seemed a little skeptical. But Carmack, knowing Eddie as well as he did, agreed to it; with the understanding that they return them immediately after returning from Little Rock that weekend.

Early that Friday morning, with all the musical instruments and drums packed into the '62 Oldsmobile, owned by their non-paid manager; they headed out for Barton Coliseum and their ultimate fame and fortune. The four of them shared a room at a motor motel in Little Rock not far from where their manager was staying, the home of his girlfriend's parents.

When they arrived at Barton somewhere in the late afternoon that Friday, they were instructed to drive around to the side of the building, where they would be able to drive into the facility and unload their equipment at the designated cubicle. When they got into the unloading area, there were indeed what appeared to be hundreds of cubicles with bands and different types of acts unloading their equipment. Now, Eddie was using a Gibson double pickup '62 model SG, cherry red solid-body guitar and the rhythm player had a '63 Fender Strat. The bass player didn't have a high-end instrument, but still it was expensive enough. They wanted to feel that their equipment was secure, especially because they were carrying a set of expensive borrowed drums. They were a little apprehensive about leaving the equipment there overnight. The security guard that was roaming around assured them that all their stuff would be safe; so after picking up their passes for the next day, off they went to the motel.

This event was set up so that the talent contest would be held during the day on Saturday, and that night there would be a concert and the announcement of the winners. There was some super talent at this event. It did not take long to see that The Four Shadows were not at the top of the class. Anyhow, they enjoyed playing that day and looked forward with great anticipation to seeing the great Bobby Bare and the even greater Johnny Tillotson that night live in person.

When they arrived back at Barton that night, they never actually took seats in the audience but remained backstage where all the contestants had their equipment stored in the cubicles. So they were right there with Bare and Tollistion as they went on stage and came off from their performances. They stood right beside Tollistion as he was waiting to go onstage and tried to talk to him but he was pretty stuck up and would not respond much to conversation. He did have this pocket comb that he would pull out of his pocket about every minute or two and comb his long dark hair, which maybe was done as a nervous reaction before he went on stage.

During the early part of the show that evening, they noticed a guy standing over by The Four Shadows' cubicle and looking at their equipment. This sort of concerned Eddie so he got their drummer to walk over there with him and talked to the guy to try and figure out what was interesting him so much. When they approached him and told him that was their stuff, he replied that he was the drummer for Bobby Bare and even shook hands with them and talked a while. He was no kid. He was probably in his 30s and had sort of what you would have called a country look to him. He noted that these were some cool cymbals they had, as he admired them. After he walked off, they went back to the area close to the stage entrance to watch Bare perform. Afterwards, they stood there and watched as Tolerton did his performance. When the concert ended, the big sliding doors of the back side of the coliseum were opened and the contestants began to load up their equipment. As they went over to their cubicle and began to load up, they found everything in place, except for this: the Zildjian cymbals. The high hat set and the two large cymbals were missing!

Oh my God, they thought, surely someone had made a mistake and taken the wrong equipment. However, by that time most of the contestants were loaded and driving off. Well, you might guess, old Bobby Bare and his band had already cleared out. They asked some of the other contestants if they had seen anyone around the equipment and they said they had seen an older guy a little bit before the show ended come over and pick up some cymbals, but they just thought he was the owner. Panic. They found a security guard who took them to the manager's office to report the theft. He advised them to call the Little Rock police and report what had happened, which they did. But, the officer said there was very little chance of finding the culprit. The Barton security and the Milk Producers organizers were entirely disinterested and Eddie learned a real good lesson of life that night.

As you may recall, youngsters find it more expedient to run from a problem than to face it head on. Ignore it and maybe it will go away is the teenager route. During the next couple days when they returned home, they paid for those cymbals with worry and tension. However, time has a way of bringing one back to reality, and by the time they were at school the next Monday, Eddie realized that there was only one solution and that was to go to Carmack directly after school and tell him the truth and put themselves at his mercy.

When school was out that afternoon, they all four went down to the Woodland Hills Real Estate office to face Carmack. Since Eddie was the one who knew him the most and had asked for the favor, he agreed to do the talking. When they got to the office, Ms. T was in the office with Carmack. She was sort of the rough and gruff type while Carmack was a relatively easy-going type of person. Anyhow, after Eddie told the story they sort of all stood there looking at each other, awaiting a response. Ms. T had a couple of innocuous questions but nothing alarming. Carmack simply said that they need not worry about it and that he would check into the matter further. Probably he either contacted the sponsors of the event and threatened a lawsuit or he had the equipment insured.

So, while The Four Shadows did not win a prize at the Teen Jamboree '65, they did have the honor of being the band whose cymbals were stolen by the great Bobby Bare and company!

Eddie and The Beatles

Ed told me this story years later. It begins the morning of Saturday, September 19, 1964. It was very bright and an unusually warm day, characteristic of the later season in the Ozarks. Eddie had started his senior year at the newly consolidated Highland School.

There was not much happening in Hardy at that time of the year. The summer tourist season was over and the beaches and the rec center at Cherokee Village were closed. All the pretty girls who came to vacation for the summer were back home in Memphis or Illinois.

At this time, TV8, the television station in Jonesboro had been on the air for a short time and was not yet affiliated with a national network. Because of this, they ran a lot of old movies and used a lot of airtime telecasting local TV shows. You may remember those days.

One of the shows they ran on Saturday was *TV8 Party*. It was the local version of *The Dick Clark Show*. A guy named Larry McAdams was the host. He was one of the suave, slicked-back hair types; the typical rich kid type, maybe the son of Herbert McAdams the wealthy businessman from Jonesboro, who owned the station at the time.

McAdams would always take the mic to announce the next record they were going to play, and sometimes make other announcements or commercial spots. Each show featured a different high school, and they would dance to the songs. Just like on *Dick Clark*.

Suddenly, McAdams broke into one of the songs with a special announcement. The way he acted; you would think the Russians had just declared war. He started by saying that something very special had happened in the early morning hours in northeast Arkansas: the Beatles were in Walnut Ridge just at daybreak. He started a film someone had shot documenting their arrival.

Sure enough, a medium sized aircraft had landed at the Walnut Ridge airport and there they were, the Beatles, disembarking from the plane, walking around and talking to bystanders. The film had been taken by a young girl who had a 35mm camera, as no one from the media knew they were coming. Apparently, it was a big surprise. Charles Snapp, who later became the mayor of Walnut Ridge, was there that morning as his father was head of the airport. The airport had been alerted after the Beatles' last concert that the group would need to land at Walnut Ridge and transfer to a smaller plane for the trip to a private retreat in Alton, Missouri. Mr. Snapp told his son, who had spread the word to a lot of kids and other residents. There was a good-sized greeting party for them when they arrived.

As Eddie watched the film that morning, he could not believe what he was seeing. He immediately ran to downtown Hardy, as he did not have a car or a phone. There was nothing going on at the pool hall where they all gathered on the weekend. No one around. So, he walked on toward the east end of town to a service station, where Eddie's good friend, Bobby Duncan, worked on weekends. Bobby was a real Beatles maniac. He later became the drummer in the second Mystics band.

Also at the station were three other friends: Bob Sherrill, The Mystics' original drummer; Dick Atkins, who was older and out of school; and Dale Stowers, one of Eddie's classmates. They were busy playing poker, using matchsticks for money. Eddie shouted out, "THE BEATLES ARE IN ALTON!" Of course, the others thought he was crazy or had been drinking beer. He tried to explain what he had seen on TV. He repeated the story again and they began to quiz him like a defense attorney would grill a murder witness. He finally told them go to hell. They went on with the card game. Occasionally one of them would say to him, "Now tell us the truth about the Beatles."

After an hour or so, Bob Sherrill told the others that he believed Eddie. He wanted to drive to Alton to see if they could find them. They all agreed, but only Duncan owned a car at that time, and he was scheduled to keep the station open for another three hours. Bob convinced Duncan that no one would know or care if the station closed early. Duncan had sold very little gas the whole day. So, just a little after 2:00, all five of them piled into Duncan's '59 Ford and headed for Alton. They all bragged to each other what they would say and do when they saw the Beatles.

Just over the state line is Thayer. There's two or three liquor stores on Highway 63. Bob had an ID that showed he was 21 (he was really 19). So, they pooled what little money they had and bought a pint of whiskey and two six-packs. They headed north on Highway 63, then Highway 19 to Alton. They were familiar with the area because of Club 19. Little Louie and the Rhythm Clowns, Richard Manning, and the Satellites had been playing there for some time and Bob and Eddie would go to listen and to sit in.

They got to Alton about 3:00, not real certain where they were going. Eddie recalled the TV announcer saying the band would be staying at the Pigman Ranch. They had never heard of it. They drove around asking people about Pigman Ranch. No luck. Eddie's friends were starting to speak of a wild goose chase. Just then he spied a small garage on the square. The door was open, a mechanic was peering under a car hood. They stopped, went inside, and asked about the ranch. To their great relief, the mechanic said he knew the ranch and gave them directions: about six or seven miles out of town, off the state highway onto a county gravel road. They found the church on the highway and made the right-hand turn as instructed. Then a long drive on a gravel road; it seemed like fifty miles. They saw nothing that resembled a ranch and thought it must be the wrong road. Then they saw several cars parked beside the road and several people standing around. There was a guarded gate on the right. They could not see what was at the top of the hill for the thick foliage. Bob, who was a quick thinker, told Duncan not to stop; to instead continue down the county road. In a few minutes, they were out of sight from the gate.

They parked beside a pasture, thinking this must be part of the ranch. Having finished off the whisky and beer, they were feeling brave. They climbed over the fence and to the top of the hill. They could see a long fence covered in hedge. They figured they were getting close to the Beatles.

Ed was worried because of the two huge bulls close by eyeballing them with suspicion. They proceeded cautiously to the hilltop, to the hedge. The hedge covered a tall chain-link fence. They sat on the ground looking at the chain-link and deciding what to do. They heard voices on the other side, so they knew someone awaited them if they climbed over.

They heard a car driving on the county road and figured they had been caught and would be arrested. A few minutes went by, nothing. They decided they might as well give it a try and started over the chain-link fence and jumped down on the other side.

Ed knew this was a once in a lifetime thing and would be worth whatever punishment might be had. With that in mind, they jumped down from the nine-foot wall in unison and landed inside the compound.

The spot they landed in was a gravel drive leading to a large farm house. About 200 feet in the opposite direction, another drive led to a swimming pool area surrounded by chain-link. At the far end of the pool sat a group of men in lounge chairs, the type you usually find at hotel pools. The men saw the boys immediately and Eddie's crew knew they were caught.

At that moment, a large man sprang up from his spot, running toward them in a frenzy while shouting at the top of his voice. At that, a thin man sprang up and spoke to the larger man and told him to relax; that he would take care of it all. Thin man motioned them over. When they got closer, Eddie could tell that it was John Lennon.

Lennon was very cordial to them and said not to be afraid. He told the boys that the Beatles were about to have a business meeting. Lennon still had on wet swim trunks with a long sleeve, ruffled shirt, typical of the British musicians of the time. Eddie could see that Paul and Ringo were two of the others in the loungers. Lennon pointed to another and told the boys, "That's Bryan Epstein." Eddie asked if George had made the trip. Lennon replied that George was in the farmhouse. The others never spoke a word to the boys, hardly acknowledged them except for an occasional glance.

They talked to John Lennon for about half an hour. He told the story of how the Beatles happened to come to the ranch that day, the history of his group and the early gigs in Hamburg. He was very interested in which artists the boys liked the most. He talked a long time about Chuck Berry. He told them that the group would be going back to Walnut Ridge Sunday morning to catch a plane to Saint Louis, eventually to New York and a final show.

Ed asked Lennon if they could just walk out along the front

entrance instead of climbing that fence again. That would be fine. What if the guards arrest us? Lennon said, "just tell him that I told you guys to come out here and it will be alright."

It was getting dark by the time they reached the front gate. Sure enough, the guards started shouting at them. Bob stuck his finger in the guard's face and told him that John Lennon gave them permission to leave through that gate. The gate opened and they walked down towards the county road. Walking out, all the fans thought they were the Beatles and had appeared to speak to them. It caused a mini riot there on the county road.

Luckily, Dale had driven around to the front gate, and was right there to pick them up. They drove back to Alton and stopped at the Club 19 for a couple of drinks and to listen to The Satellites. At break, Eddie approached Richard Manning and told him about the Beatles. Manning didn't believe him. He did let Eddie and Bob sit in for a few numbers. Eddie announced to the crowd what they had just witnessed just a few miles away. All the locals were pretty well-lit and shouted him down. They yelled, "Play *Johnny B. Goode*, play *Arkansas Twist*." They would not believe that the greatest rock stars in the world could be just a few miles away from their favorite honkytonk.

JAMES

I met James around age 15. James was from a musical family, he played guitar and so did all his brothers. He had a very good band with James on bass and brother David on lead. James had recruited a skilled saxophone player, Joe, and great drummer, Donald. Their band had played around, but I had not had the chance to see them.

James had decided to expand the lineup. He wanted to play rhythm to Dave's lead and to recruit a bass player and

a singer. One day, James asked me if I knew how to play the bass. Though I didn't even know what a bass was, I told him yes, sure I could play it. He told me to come over after school and he would show me some bass runs. In a couple of weeks, I went to Beale Street in Memphis and bought a pawn shop bass for fifteen dollars. I was in the music business.

Overnight, my grades dropped from honor student to Ds and Fs while I spent hours on bass practice. We got hot. We started making good money playing around town and the nearby honky-tonks. The year was 1964 and things will never be as sweet. I was working at the local radio station and playing music most weekends with my band, the Strait Jackets.

One of my friends was Steve. He was a personality expanded to the maximum. Because of his outlandish behavior, we called him Wild Man. He came to every practice and every gig and started calling himself "Background Screamer for the Strait Jackets." One Saturday night Wild Man went to a dance in nearby Jonesboro and came back talking about the great time he had. He urged us all to check it out when next weekend rolled around. Saturday evening, we iced a case of beer in the trunk and took off. We pulled up to the Hotel Noble, downtown by the bus station and the old jail. The parking lot was full, so we parked out on the street.

The hotel had a large hall that it rented out. The hall was packed that night. A local band, The Allstars, was playing. It became evident that the Strait Jackets needed to book the hall right away. I went to the front desk and booked it for two weeks down the road. We were all excited about the prospect. During the next few days, we went to Jonesboro and hung signs (we later found out that all our signs were ripped down by another band). Two Saturdays later we went to Jonesboro and kicked it out. We gave it everything we had. We made a lot of money and got great reviews. Of course, we booked Hotel Noble again.

DONALD

I never really knew Donald until I started playing music with him our junior year in high school. We became very close friends. He was a talented drummer at a young age, and his parents encouraged him in that regard. They volunteered their living room as practice space and helped in any other way they could. They certainly doted on Donald. We had such a great time practicing and gigging around most every weekend. It seemed we had the world by the tail. Everything came so easily for us. In a short time, we had a really hot band. This was just before the advent of the Beatles, and when they hit, they lifted every other band into the stratosphere.

Gus, Donald's father, agreed to buy him a new car for his birthday, and to let him choose which car to get. In 1964, Chevrolet marketed an entirely new model: Chevelle Malibu.

The one Donald wanted was a baby blue, 357 v8. He ordered one with cutouts so that the exhaust could be manually opened to produce that wonderful racking sound and made the car go a bit faster too. A more magnificent automobile, I have never seen. Gus only asked one thing in return. He wanted to leave the car stock, thereby making it easier to sell or trade in a few years. Donald initially agreed to that. Later, after he got the Chevelle Malibu, Donald changed his mind about it. The car did not come with a tachometer; Donald thought he must have one. Father and son had several heated arguments about the matter, and it was left unresolved. To everyone else it seemed such a small matter.

One day James and I were driving down Main Street, and spied Donald walking in the opposite direction on the sidewalk. We pulled over and he got in. Donald said, "Well, Doc really spoiled my party. He wouldn't fill my prescription." Doc Clayton, the local pharmacist, would not fill his out-of-date prescription. We drove along and talked.

Out of the blue, Donald told us that he had been thinking about the best way to kill himself. Besides overdose, he had thought about going as fast as he could in the new car and crashing it into a tree. Yes, we should have warned someone about his mood; but at sixteen, this all just sailed right over our heads. Our response to all of this was to try to cheer him up with talk about the gig we had the next weekend at Hotel Noble. We made sure that he would show up that night at the poker game we had planned. He said yes, he would be there. That evening in the conversation around the table, Donald said that he was leaving town soon. We asked where he was going, we would go with him. He told us no, where he was going we could not go. We could not understand just what he was saying, although it later became so obvious.

Setting around the poker table, we hatched a plan. We would

all leave town en masse right after we got paid for the coming gig. The most exotic place in the world we could imagine was Biloxi, so that became the plan. The entire band would travel to Biloxi after the Hotel Noble gig on Saturday. Everyone, including Donald, agreed to this unlikely course of action.

The next day I went to work at the radio station and my boss explained to me that I was going to run a promotion that afternoon. The Beatles had just released their first movie, *Hard Day's Night*, and everyone was anxious to see it. The theater in Jonesboro (about 15 miles to the northwest) gave the station several tickets to a special screening of the film. I announced this and people started calling in; every twentieth person would get two tickets. Donald was one of the winners. He told me he would be right over. When Donald showed, he seemed in a much better mood than the night before, laughing and joking. He was very excited about the tickets and said he was looking forward to the Beatles event. Then he left and that was the last time I ever saw him alive.

That evening, I was at home when the phone rang. A classmate, Leroy, was on the line. Leroy told me that he had heard that Donald had been shot and was in the clinic downtown. He wanted to know if that was true. My first thought was that word had gotten out about Donald's plan to take some pills and that had spawned some wild rumors. I jumped in my car and raced the mile to the clinic. Just as I pulled up, the deputy sheriff was exiting the building. He told me that Donald had just expired from a self-inflicted gunshot. A ton of bricks fell down on me.

That night there was a crowd at Donald's home, they came to share sympathy and to help any way they could. Donald's buds sat on the front porch with his parents, Gus and Polly. After a time, Gus said, "I know there are people here tonight that could have prevented this if only they would have said something to someone." He pointed at James and me. Polly said, "Gus, don't say things like that. Put yourself in their shoes. Don't blame them, they didn't want to get him in trouble is all."

Donald was buried on his seventeenth birthday. The band members were the pallbearers. We found out later that Gus had secretly bought a tachometer to surprise Donald on his birthday.

For years I dreamed about Donald. One dream is particularly vivid in my mind. I was in the variety store on Main Street, with many items on long shelves. In the dream, I caught a glimpse of Donald turning down an aisle. He seemed to be avoiding me, kept moving from aisle to aisle playing a hiding game. Finally, I cornered him and talked to him. I asked him, "What is it like to be dead?" In my dream, Donald smiled and replied, "It's like everything else. It gets old after a while."

STRAIT JACKETS LAST GIG

After Donald's death, the band seemed to be so unimportant. We were all drifting, aimless. But then James recruited Dennis to play drums and things started to turn.

Dennis was a great drummer, a pro even in high school. He played almost every week at the Cotton Club. As a favor to James, he came aboard. With graduation approaching, we made plans to play proms and such. We were playing a school dance in the town's Community House one night that fall.

David played the guitar in the band. He was deeply in love with his girlfriend, Mary, and was very jealous. If he saw her even talking to anyone, he would go off on a tear. Funny, this occurrence is just like the script of a movie I once saw. We were halfway through a Chuck Berry song and the dance floor was packed. David looked down at the dancers and saw, to his chagrin, his beloved Mary dancing with another man. Dave's smiling face became a contorted mess. He jerked off his Gibson guitar, threw it onto the stage and smashed it to bits. He turned to the band and made his intention known. He said, "I'll never play the guitar again." As far as I know, he never did.

David and Mary got married and lived a long and prosperous life together. Both Dave and his brother, James, became Baptist preachers. The sax player was Joe; the drummer, Dennis. I ran into Dennis not so long ago and we talked about the band. Dennis told me that Joe had taken a job with the Godfather, James Brown, but that lately things had not gone well with him, that I should call him and cheer him up. When he answered his phone he talked in a sluggish manner; he sounded drunk. It took the longest time to get him to remember who I was. Finally, he did and we were able to have a conversation. As a joke I told him that we should get the band back together and play at the upcoming class reunion. He said that would be great. His voice changed a bit and then had a faraway dreamlike tint to it. Joe said, "That would give me something to live for." A few days later I got the news that Joe had died.

Since Strait Jackets, I must have been in some hundred or more bands. I saw seven years with Ocie, twenty years with Luda! What I learned from the Strait Jackets was that music (at least for me) should not be a serious thing. Rather, it should be something to be enjoyed just for its own sake. That's the attitude I have tried to maintain (though sometimes I forget and start getting serious about it again).

BURGER AND THE NEW ESQUIRES

Burger's time in Jonesboro has always been somehow passed over. But I was in two different bands with Burger when we were students at Arkansas State University. In one of these bands, we played three gigs in Jonesboro and in the Missouri bootheel. This was in the year 1967, which was a very good year for bands and for partying in general, what with the sexual revolution and the great records that were coming out at the time.

Burger and I had teamed up with Chip and were practicing for a big debut for Lemon Meat but for the appearance of the Swan and the Raven. These two were also students at ASU and had plans of their own about getting a band together. Swan was my roommate on Danny Drive (named after Danny Brewer), by the Jami Bee Motel on Nettleton Avenue. Danny Drive is a cul de sac and thereby was the scene of several street parties and assorted other goings on (e.g., Joe Vaughan and the notorious Dippy Doo Incident). The Swan was always scheming up some big deal to make some easy money; one of these schemes was putting bands together and throwing dances. The Raven was just back from the Marines and the two had become partners, along with Frank Angelo, in several unseemly activities. Luckily, they were both good musicians as well.

Somehow the Swan and the Raven talked Burger and me into forgetting about Chip and instead joining their group. We

rented an old sharecropper house near Hergett as our practice house. It was wintertime so each time we practiced everyone had to bring some firewood to start a fire in the wood stove we had installed. Soon the small structure was full of our collection of amps, instruments and such.

Then, of course, we agonized over what to name the band, a big consideration at the time. We went through several sessions without consensus. Raven had been in another Jonesboro band named The Esquires. He still had stacks and stacks of posters from that band. These posters were the good ones, made of stiff cardboard and with lots of color. So, we became the New Esquires to cash in on this resource.

In a few weeks (or maybe it was a few days) of practice we figured we were ready for prime time. Swan got us three gigs, one right after the next. One was in Jonesboro (he rented the Holiday Inn); one was in Kennett, Missouri (his fraternity brothers rented the Top Hat Club) and one was at the Batman A-Go-Go in Cape Girardeau (famous for a UFO crash there in the early sixties). It was our big, and only, tour.

My recollection of Burger from those days has stayed with me ever since. He played a white Telecaster at the time. It was a cool guitar. He carried a bottle of furniture polish and kept it sitting on his amp. Before each song he would literally pour furniture polish on his guitar's neck and strings and on his chord hand. He claimed the lubrication helped him to quickly move over the strings. I've never seen anyone do that before or since.

Another thing Burger did was really funny. During that time aspiring musicians would come up and stand right in front of the bandstand, watching the players to learn their riffs. Burger would goof on these guys. If he noticed that someone was watching his cord changes, he would start making nonsense cords, making up new cords and inverting real cords into upside down gibberish. The funny thing was that when he did this, he never missed a beat and it always sounded good. Go figure. He got some unusual reactions from the gawkers.

The New Esquires didn't last very long. As a matter of fact, its demise was right after the big tour and was the result of one of Swan's and Raven's scams.

One day I got a call from the Swan. He had bad news. Someone had broken into the practice house and had stolen a bunch of the equipment. I asked him: "What about my amp and guitar?" "They didn't take your stuff," he told me. "They only took mine and Raven's stuff." It was obvious to me what had transpired, but apparently it wasn't obvious to the insurance company that had the equipment covered. Anyway, that was the end of that.

The Swan went on to bigger and better scams. The Raven became a land baron. For many years I lost track of Burger until he came to Fayetteville to play at Lilly's on Dickson Street as Burger and Friends around 1986. I went to hear the band and they were great. One thing I noticed was that Burger didn't play any upsidedown cords. He had mellowed a bit over the years. I had a good time talking over old times with him later.

I kept in close touch with Swan after the band. I would occasionally run into him. He dropped out of school and returned to his hometown to start a family with his new bride. One sunny day, he and three friends went boat riding on the White River. One striking feature of the river in that stretch is a massive spillway. When the White is up, there can be a strong torrent coming over the spillway.

The story goes that Swan gave his life vest to a young lady, so he continued the adventure without one. When the party reached the middle of the river, the motor started to sputter — out of gas. The river was high that day, its water swirling over the spillway. As the current started to pull the boat toward the abyss, the three others dove in and swam to the safety of shore, all except Swan. He stayed with the boat as it went over and was never seen again. Or was he?

In the months and years after his death, there were reports of his sighting. One person that I believe to be trustworthy described to me this occurrence:

"I went to Las Vegas on vacation. I always play the craps, that is my game. I was doing well, a crowd gathered around the table. At one point, I glanced around a bit when I saw the Swan walk up to the table. I am sure it was him, he flashed me that Swan smile. I had to make a roll, then when I looked back, he was gone."

I have my own opinions about the matter and have come to some conclusions. There are several issues that tell me Swan survived that day.

1. SWAN'S PAST: I personally saw him pull one scam after the other. I gotta say this sounds like something he would do.

2. STRONG FEAR OF THE WATER: He was my roommate for a long time. In that situation, you get to know someone well. I know for a fact that the Swan was afraid of the water. A lazy jaunt on the river sounds so out of character.

3. CHIVALROUS SWAN: He gave his life vest to a young lady. Chivalry is a side I never saw of Swan.

4. NO CORPUS: Several people have gone over the spillway. Some survived, some did not. Swan is the only person to go over where a body was never subsequently found.

5. DOUBLE INDEMNITY: Swan worked for several years in the insurance business. He knew the ins and outs.

I was enjoying breakfast in a café in Calico Rock one morning not long after the Swan's demise. I noticed a gentleman from my hometown and invited him to sit for a bit. He told me that he was on his way to Batesville to deliver a check to the widow of "the boy who drowned." The check, he told me, was in the amount of $70,000 (a fortune at that time). I know that Swan was under heavy debt at the time of his death. 2+2=5.

With all this said, I do believe that Swan is indeed deceased; no matter how much his friends want him back.

I ran into the Raven in that same café in Calico Rock. He

looked a bit down, so I took a seat at his table to talk about the old times. Instead, he wanted to talk about his girlfriend. Raven was a real lady's man. He always had a pretty girl on his arm. When he met Val, everything changed for him. He fell in love. The problem was that Val did not feel the same. Raven could not get over Val. That day at the café, Raven bared his soul. Val had left and he did not know how he could bear it. On top of that, he was heavily in debt and had a balloon payment approaching. He was down and out, but I tried to cheer him up as best I could.

A few days later, I got the news from Angelo that the Raven was gone; had jumped, or had fallen off the Calico Rock bluff, sixty feet down to the railroad track below.

And now Burger has left the building too. I lost some good friends along the way, but what I did get to keep were many good memories of those friends. Sometimes I wonder why I am the only one left. I think it's because I can dance.

BEALE STREET

I would usually skip English and Trigonometry classes with JR during our senior year in high school. Instead, we would drive the short distance to Memphis, then head to Beale Street. At the time, the area was rundown, old and tired. But now Furry Lewis is gone, and so is the urban blight. The City of Memphis got funds from the Fed to renovate. Now the area is a Disneyland for drunks. Way back when though, it was great just to be standing there.

Sure enough, Lewis sat right there on the sidewalk. A cup sat near him for tips. He played an old Stella guitar. To the Stella six-string he had added a seventh string. His slide was an RC bottle. We walked on down to the east end of Beale Street and had a Coke at the dry goods store.

One long line of Beale Street's shops was all pawn shops. That's where we would spend a lot of time looking at the musical instruments but not buying.

At the time, Gibson guitars had a factory on Beale Street. What a sight their showroom window was.

At the end of the street was Lansky Brothers, a haberdashery. They had the coolest threads by far. It's where Elvis used to shop. Does anyone remember Nehru jackets?

Leaving Beal then walking north you see Madison Steet, an unassuming storefront is Sonic Studio, Roland Jayne's studio. Roland was Sam Phillips' (Sun Records) right hand. I did some recording there with Saturday's Children. I found out recently that the Swan was working with Roland on an album there when he disappeared. But for me, it all started at the Maxie.

TOMMY

My sister, Jane, gave me a book about John Lennon one Christmas. It tells the story of the Beatles' last American tour in 1966. The account relates the story of their gig in Memphis. All of those British stars wanted to play in Memphis and to go down to Beale Street and look for Furry Lewis. During those times, I could drive the 40 miles to Memphis and see the crème de la crème of the era; the ones who became real legends. The ticket prices we paid to see those bands are hilarious now. I saw the Beatles for $4.50, and about that same price for Jimi too.

The book relates that everyone there could sense the tension in the air that day in Memphis. This feeling increased when someone in the audience threw lit fireworks toward the stage. John Lennon had really made some folks angry with his statement about the Beatles being "more popular than Jesus." They were up in arms, particularly in the Bible Belt. The Beatles' management was skittish at the idea of playing Memphis, as they had received several menacing notes and phone calls. When their bus pulled into the Mid-South Coliseum, the entire entourage ducked down in their seats, worried about snipers. According to Jane's book, during the performance, someone in the audience threw fireworks at the stage. For a moment everything stopped. In a few seconds, the band started playing again and made it through the set. Reading about this incident really brought back memories almost forgotten over time. Here is my own story of the last Beatles concert in Memphis.

This was a big deal for me and my friends, as we were all fans of the band. A friend had bought several tickets before the show sold out. He kept two and had no problem in selling the others. JR and I had a hot band and a real interest in the Beatles. Another friend, Tommy, offered to take his car for the drive to Memphis. The appointed time came, but JR was nowhere to be seen. Tommy and I took off anyway. Tommy drove a 1955 Chevy. Though now it is such a collectable car, at the time it was a real heap. But Memphis was so close by, we were not so worried.

On the road trip, we talked. Tommy said, "You know, it's funny. Sometimes I say something bad might happen, then it does." He went on to provide examples. Once he was double-dating and, of course, they were cruising the dusty back roads of Poinsett County. So far so good, but he did not have a spare tire. Tommy said to his date mates, "Do you know what would be really terrible?" They allowed not. "What if we got way back in the boonies and got a flat tire?" In a few minutes, sure enough, flat tire and way back in the boonies. They all walked home.

After Tommy told me his story, he thought for a while. He finally said, "Do you know what would be terrible?"

"No, what?"

"What if we got all the way to the Mid-South Coliseum, right out in the main intersection, and my car would quit? What would we do?" After he said that, we sat in silence again.

Soon we could see the bridges across the Mississippi River. The traffic was thick that day, my friend. The closer we got to the coliseum, the thicker it got. Finally, we were in sight of our destination. We inched up to the turn lane that would lead into the parking lot.

Meanwhile, in the middle of the giant parking lot, the local Ku Klux Klan was present and accounted for in their full regalia. In the middle of those assembled was a 55-gallon barrel. The well-tended fire in the barrel was fueled by Beatles records. Inside the venue were 18,000 screaming fans.

Just when we got under the main traffic light, the car stalled. Steam started pouring out from under our hood. We got out and stood and looked. Meanwhile the traffic started backing up in both directions. It looked like the beginning of a major traffic jam with car horns blaring. We had a decision to make, miss the concert and deal with this mess or abandon the car and walk two hundred yards to see the Beatles.

Tommy and I found our seats in the mezzanine section. We had great seats right next to the railing, one floor up from stage level, cantilevered over the seats below. JR's seat sat empty. I found out a little later he was in jail at the time and could not make it.

The Mid-South Coliseum is just the opposite of a well-designed music hall such as the Ryman. The coliseum looks like two flying saucers landed: two giant concrete bowls, one inverted on the other. The acoustics in the building are just terrible. You can imagine the sound of several loud electric instruments, all turned to 11, bounced and rebounded in this concrete orb. Add to that the roar of a hysterical crowd.

The music started with Sam the Sham and the Pharaohs. They all came out in tuxes and in turbans. It was pretty cheesy. Sam the Sham had the number two hit in the nation that week with *Wooly Bully*. Not long before this concert, I met Sam (his real name is Domingo Samudio) as he made the rounds of local radio stations promoting his records. Now, just a few weeks later, he was opening for the Beatles.

After Sam's short set came the Remains, a Boston outfit. The Beatles tour was their only eight-week claim to fame. They became "America's greatest lost band." They delivered a good set. Then it was time for the Beatles.

Pandemonium broke loose. They started the set, but it was impossible to hear very much of the songs over the incredible roar. It built up velocity as it flew round and round the coliseum.

A few songs into the set, Tommy leaned over and shouted into my ear, "Watch this." With that he reached into his pocket and pulled out a cherry bomb and a cigarette lighter. These cherry bombs were much different than any fireworks one could buy today. They really packed a punch. They were loud. Tommy lit the fuse and lobbed the cherry bomb over the mezzanine rail. I can still see this in my mind's eye: the cherry bomb appeared to move in slow motion, as if caught in a strobe light's beam in a perfect arch over the main floor of the venue. With a loud report it exploded, and everything halted in that instant. The roar stopped. The music stopped. You could hear a pin drop in the massive concrete structure.

Lennon was standing to the back of the stage by Ringo; the others turned to look, expecting him to have been shot. This all seemed to happen in a prolonged state, though it really was only two seconds. Then as a unit, the band hit the beat and continued *Johnny B. Goode*, and not missing a note. Roar. These days if someone did something like Tommy did, they would end up in jail. But that was a totally different time. No one said a word to us about it.

Half an hour later with the concert over, we filed out wondering about what we would find when we got back to the intersection and the abandoned car. As we walked closer, we could see that the car was long gone, and traffic whizzed by unencumbered. We stood there on the street corner wondering where the Chevy was and how we were going to get back home. Just then a car pulled to the curb, and someone yelled. It was Steve, a mutual friend. He had been to the concert and happened to see us standing there on the street. We climbed in. The next day Tommy went back to Memphis and retrieved his car from police impound.

After that, the years passed the door.

I cannot get in touch with Tommy now, even in the age of social media. I wish I could. He is avoiding all his old friends, but for a very good reason.

JR became a Baptist minister. I have a mind to go visit him. Maybe we could talk about the Beatles.

PAUL

I've been knowing Paul for a long time; many years. He died not so long ago. Paul was certainly one of my best friends. Time was when I considered him my brother. Then life happened and I lost track of him. Turns out we lived close by for much of that time. I met Paul through music, of course. We both attended ASU. Paul's band was Saturday's Children. They all were studying music and were excellent players. Saturday's Children had a strong following in the tri-state area. They were making money. Their bass player decided to move back to Saint Louis and had left them with a full list of bookings. I auditioned and got the job. For about two years in the late '60s, we gigged hard every weekend.

Somehow, I reestablished contact with Paul years later and we continued our friendship. We even played three jazz gigs with Luda. Turns out that Paul had made music his career, playing with many notables, from Jacky Wilson to the Platters.

One day I got a phone call from Paul. He was in the hospital, could I come and get him? I told him I'd be right over. When I got there, he was just about to be discharged. I helped him carry his belongings to the car. He told me a sorrowful story. His family had kicked him out of the house. Paul asked me if he could stay at my house for a while. I told him sure, but that in two weeks, we were set to leave town; he would have to make other arrangements after that. We were all set.

Paul stayed with us for the next two weeks. We had a great time, jamming and such. Paul had an electric guitar with him. It was a beautiful red Gibson; it had a very nice sound. He told me the story of its acquisition.

Around 1966, a Memphis band, the Hombres, had a regional hit with a record called *Let It All Hang Out.* Paul's Gibson had belonged to a member of that band. It had a real nice Gibson tone to it, and we enjoyed jamming with it.

Time passed, we went to Montego Bay and Paul went to live with his brother in Texas. After we returned home, I thought about our visit with Paul, and started thinking about that song, *Let it All Hang Out.* It has a crazy introduction, a preacher admonishing us regarding "nicotine, John Barleycorn and the temptations of Eve." When I heard that line in my mind, it sounded like a song title: *Nicotine, John Barleycorn and Temptations of Eve.*

I thought about some of the songs of others I had covered. There is a song that I have played many times and in many bands; *Don't Stop Believing* by Journey. I never liked the song (or that band) very much, but there was something I noticed about that song. Any time we would kick it off, everyone within ear shot would drop whatever they were doing and would start getting into the song. People loved that song. Everyone knows the lyrics and will start singing along: audience participation.

I remembered another song that affects the audience in the same way; the song by Clapton, *Cocaine*. When a band plays that song live, everyone there knows when to chime in on the chorus. With these thoughts in mind, I looked again at the title I had discovered. I tried this in my head: Cocaine, John Barleycorn and Temptations of Eve. Voila! It's a two-step song about the prodigal son. Like they say, "the song wrote itself."

Not long after that, I received a letter from Paul. He asked me if the two weeks he was here were great; did it result in any song ideas? I corresponded back and told him about my thought process I have just described to you. I told him he had song writing credits, along with the Crooze Brothers, Baba and Coy Ray.

In a few days, I got an email from Paul's brother, Bruce. Paul had deceased.

There are a lot of Paul memories in the song, that's one reason I like it so much. This effort is also dedicated to the memory of the Holy Roller.

Temptations of Eve is in the key of A, tempo is 74. Harps are A/E. 3/4 time, I try to put one in each album. The lyrics seem to really roll. "Cocaine, John Barleycorn and Temptations of

Eve." Note several turnarounds in the song.

The song is a confession, a remembrance. The prodigal begs forgiveness, then starts to preach.

CHARLEY RICH'S CADDY

When you are a musician, you will quickly learn not to loan out your delicate (and expensive) musical equipment. I mean not to anyone.

Charley Rich was born and raised in a small farming community near Memphis. From infancy, he was a musical savant. When he came of age, he left home and decided to go to Memphis to find his fortune. Charley hitchhiked the twenty miles to Shelby County.

He was let out on Beale Street and walked the few remaining blocks to Sun Records, on Union, determined to be granted a shot at an audition. He soon found the studio, but the lady said Sam Phillips was not there yet. Charley allowed he would wait.

He sat around a bit then grabbed a broom from the corner of the room. He started sweeping. Charley thought about what he would say to Sam when he got the chance. He kept sweeping.

Finally, a shiny red Cadillac pulled up to the curb. Sam stepped out and walked into the fabled recording studio, where he encountered a young hillbilly boy sweeping furiously. When Charley saw Sam, he demanded an audition. Charley was surprised when Sam said (without hesitation), "OK." Charley was in rare form and blew Sam away that day. They signed the standard contract and Charley started writing songs. He had a couple of regional hits then drifted for a while, playing the clubs around town.

One morning Charley came in with a new song called *Lonely Weekends*. Roland Jaynes helped to smooth out the edges, then they were ready to record. Soon the song was a national hit, and in rotation on all the stations.

Fast Forward.

Early one Saturday morning, I got a phone call from the

music store. "Would you please come over and bring your rig. It's an emergency. Charley Rich is playing at State tonight and needs to borrow your stuff. Please hurry over." I loaded up my amp and guitar and drove the short distance to the music store. I had a beautiful rig at the time, a Fender Bassman amplifier and a cherry red Gibson SG bass guitar. Double cutaways. I loved that guitar.

When I pulled up to the music store, parked in front was a brand new, white Cadillac convertible. Beside it stood ole Silver Fox himself, Charley Rich. I got out and introduced myself. We stood there sharing small talk and started moving the equipment into the Caddy. Charley said he would leave town the following day around noon. I would be at Paul's at that time and gave him directions. It would be on his way out of town. I knew that I was violating my own rules about lending out music equipment, but hey, this was Charley Rich.

That night there came a torrential downpour, but the next day was cloudless and beautiful. I was at Paul's, and he was very excited that he was about to meet Charley. Noon came and went but no Charley. But what do you expect from a star? One o'clock, no Charley. Two, three o'clock, nothing. I was getting nervous.

Suddenly there was a loud commotion coming from the back. We all ran outside to look. Directly behind Paul's back yard was a cotton patch still wet and muddy from the night's rain. In the middle of the field of knee-high cotton was the white Caddy slinging gumbo mud and roaring as Charley tried his best to continue to inch on forward toward Paul's dry gravel drive just ahead. He was jerking the steering wheel from side to side to keep the car's momentum rocking forward. Despite the soft gumbo mud, he was getting closer to the end of the patch. When he reached the turn row, he revved the engine high. The Caddy responded and seemed to climb up and onto the dry drive. He made it, but his car was a real mess.

Charley seemed in a hurry and there wasn't much to say. We unloaded the equipment onto the driveway. He jumped into the car and started the engine. He reached into the back seat and pulled out a six pack of Bud; he handed it to me. Then he drove off towards Highway 63 and Memphis.

A few days passed and I needed to get ready for a job the next weekend. When I opened the guitar case, out came the guitar in two pieces, someone had dropped it on the floor and had broken the neck in two. Ruined, unrepairable. I was heart-broken, and I haven't got over it yet. I've tried to contact Charley by phone; I haven't been able to. I've sent letters; no reply. The good news is that I got my hands on a wonderful Fender Precision Bass, 1970s model, made in the USA. I'm using an Ampeg amplifier with it and these two things together constitute the best rig in town. Guess what? I never loan it out.

BOBBY LEE TRAMMEL

Times have changed in northeast Arkansas. It is difficult to believe that there used to be such a thriving music scene. Now, efforts are underway to designate a stretch of US Highway 67, from Newport to Walnut Ridge, as the Rockabilly Highway. Indeed, things were really jumping there once upon a time. Venues such as The Silver Moon, Porky's Rooftop, King's Capri, these were real hot spots come the weekend.

Highway 63 slices 67 at Walnut Ridge, and journeys on toward Memphis; the motherload of true Rockabilly. The music legends from Sun Records would drive the few miles down 63 to entertain the local hoi polloi in the two night clubs of Trumann: The Cotton Club and the C&R. They all played the C&R in its heyday: Carl, Johnny, Jerry Lee. These cats inspired many of the local wannabes to take up the guitar in the effort to escape the hot cotton patches. One of these wannabes was Bobby Lee Trammel.

Trammel was from the nearby community of Hergett, just across the county line. Hergett is not even on the map anymore. Now he is gone, with no one left to sing his song. But during his salad days, he did his best to shake things up. His live show was certainly something to see. Bobby Lee would literally swing from the rafters as he belted out his tunes. He rode around shirtless on the back of his bass player while singing *Johnny B. Goode*. The crowd erupted.

Bobby Lee's biggest hit record was undoubtedly *Arkansas Twist*, which he recorded in 1963. He teamed up with Joe Lee, a legend in his own right. For many years, Joe ran Alley Records and recorded local talent. Cashing in on the latest national dance craze, Bobby Lee and Joe went into Alley Studio and recorded *Arkansas Twist*. Right away it became a regional hit, but soon went even higher.

Dick Biondi worked late night radio on Chicago's WLS. WLS was directional and aimed its 50,000 watts of good will straight down the nation's midsection into Mexico. What a night it was when Biondi played Bobby Lee's song on the nation's number one radio station!

Bobby Lee went on *Top Ten Dance Party* on WHBQ-TV to do *Arkansas Twist*. Every Saturday evening at 6, George Kline (professional Elvis friend) would host the program. It featured local recording talent and a different area high school each week. The artists would lip-sync their latest record for the viewers.

A few seconds into *Arkansas Twist* and Bobby Lee had given up all pretense of the lip-sync. He regressed into his stage alter ego, climbed all over the set and rode the cameras around like bumper cars. The kids in the studio cheered him on. By the end of the song, the studio was thoroughly trashed and cast asunder. George Kline just stood there shaking his head in disbelief while Bobby Lee walked away laughing. Kline never invited him back.

In 1968 Bobby Lee decided to parlay his name recognition into a political career. He had some recent run-ins with the Craighead County Sherriff's Department and was out for revenge. The then sherriff, Lonnie Cooper, was campaigning for reelection. Bobby Lee allowed that that race would be a fine place to start his efforts. No doubt about it, Bobby Lee was up against a powerful county-wide political cartel, headed by Jonesboro lawyer, Tuffy Howard. Bobby Lee was getting nowhere with his campaign. He decided to risk everything on a half-hour telecast on local TV station, KAIT. It was perhaps his best performance.

His political platform was that John Law should stop pulling people over just to ask them who they are and where they are going.

At the dramatic conclusion of his telecast, Bobby Lee started sobbing. He told his audience, "There are some people that don't want me in this race. Me and my family have received death threats if I don't drop out. But I won't! I have no rich backers. I had to sell my tour bus just to buy this time on TV." At this revelation, the tears really started to flow. "They don't want you to have a choice in this election. WELL, AIN'T THAT JUST TUFFY!"

Bobby Lee only got 28 votes in the election. One of them was mine. But this did not stop his political aspirations one bit.

A few years later, he was elected to the Craighead County Quorum Court; then as State Representative for District 88 in 1997.

When Bobby Lee was elected to the State Legislature, his first thought was to purchase a beautiful new red pickup to drive to Little Rock. He was proud of that truck.

On his way to the session in his new job, Bobby Lee parked directly in front of the Capitol Building. A few hours later he exited, exhausted from a day of legislating. He looked around for his truck, only to find it had been stolen from its parking spot. He never saw the truck again. Welcome to Little Rock.

Bobby Lee's focus while in the legislature surrounded a terrible and destructive problem specifically haunting his home area: methamphetamine. He set to work crafting legislation addressing this scourge. His proposed law would empower John Law to shoot on sight any person who, in the estimation of the officer, might be cooking meth. Several colleagues pulled him aside to explain why this might not be a good idea.

Now the years have passed the door and things have changed in Poinsette County. The C&R Club is a storage shed for rusty farm equipment. The Cotton Club is only a charred concrete slab out on old Highway 63, miles from the new bypass. Johnny, Elvis and Carl have all left the building.

CHARLEY BELL

I went to high school with Charley Bell, I knew him when I saw him. We traveled in different circles. But I was quite familiar with Charley's brother; everyone called him "Ding." Ding worked at Sid's Pool Hall racking pool tables.

Sid had only one arm. Regardless, he was the best pool shot in the area. He was a good buddy of my father, John. They were duck hunters and went hunting every chance they got.

All John's friends called me "Johnny." One day, when I was in the middle of a pool game, Sid asked me in a loud voice, "Johnny, how old are you?" I replied, "I'm seventeen, Sid." He nodded his head as if his thoughts had been confirmed and then continued, "Seventeen years ago I was duck hunting with John. That entire day he seemed quiet and introspective.

Finally, I said to him, John, what's wrong, you haven't said two words all day. John looked chagrined and said, 'Sid, I've got my wife pregnant.'" Sid pointed his finger at me and said (even in a louder voice), "And it was you!" Everybody got a real charge out of the story and had a laugh, but I didn't mind.

The first time I met Charley Bell was quite an occasion. The Strait Jackets were playing at the grand opening of a supermarket in Jonesboro. This was the first time I ever got paid for a musical performance and my first performance with this band in public.

We had a wonderful venue; a large crowd had assembled in the massive parking lot. The stage was a flatbed truck under a starry sky. We were stoked and dove into the first set. In about an hour, we announced a short break. Things were going well. When we jumped off the stage, up walked Charley Bell. He complimented us for a good set and asked James if he could sit in. James told him yes.

Soon it was time. Charley climbed up on stage and found a guitar to strap on. He started playing a popular song: *Needles and Pens* by a British band, the Searchers. He really hit it out of the park, people cheered, a most excellent job. He played a couple more and climbed down.

The years passed the door.

The next and last time I saw Charley was at a class reunion. He was dressed in a red velvet tuxedo and had a pretty girl on his arm. We shook hands and exchanged pleasantries. Charley told me that he was putting together a tour, would I join it? I told him that I didn't think I could make it, but thanks for the offer anyway.

A few weeks later my phone rang late at night (actually really early in the morning, 2 a.m.). On the other end was Charley asking again if I would go on tour. Once again, I told him that I couldn't, maybe some other time. Charley started pleading with me. He started sobbing. I told him that he should lie down for a while, and I hung up. Click. I went back to bed and tried to go back to sleep, but without much luck.

Eddie has another Charley Bell story. He tells it in his own words:

Eddie and Charley Bell AKA Benny Bell
(As told by Eddie)

"If I recall right, it was in the spring of '64, and I was playing in a band from Hardy, called The Mystics. It was composed of myself, who sang, played rhythm and some lead; Bob the drummer and singer; Carol Ray, the lead player; and Jay, the bass player. I think the manager of the C&R Club had known Carol Ray from his days at Arkansas State University. And, knowing he had a band, had called to get us to replace a band who had to cancel for some reason.

Well, I was only 16 years old and would not turn 17 until late July, so my mother was very much against me going down there to play that gig. However, Carol Ray was 21 and Jay, who was a high school journalism teacher, was about 30. After a bit of assurance and convincing, Mom agreed to let me go with the band to play at the C&R Club.

Although we did not tell my mother, we knew the C&R had the reputation as being a pretty rough place, so I must confess that I was a little scared to go. As you probably remember, it was the thrill of playing that controlled us and I guess that, at that time in my life, I would have played in Hell if given the opportunity. Now, we were all set to leave that day, and Jay, the bass player, came down sick and was not able to go; and it looked as if we would have to back out. But lucky for us, there was a man named Louis who played bass with a local country band who were actually pretty good and had played on stage with some named country stars, like the Wilburn Brothers, Grandpa Jones and some others.

Our lead player, Carol Ray, had played some with them and was a close friend with Louis and he wound up talking Louis into filling in with us that night. I don't believe it took much arm twisting to get Louis to go because he loved to drink and honky tonk. Also, he had just bought a brand new, expensive, Fender bass guitar and wanted to show it off a bit. So there we go, off to Trumann to play in one of the top honky tonks of America.

Carol Ray had a hot rod '56 two-door Chevy and he, me and Louis left together; toting all the equipment in the trunk and back seat. Sherrill came in his own car with his girlfriend, who was going to spend the night at a hotel in Jonesboro. When we arrived, I recall coming into the club and walking right up to the bar. There was a big bartender there to greet us and I supposed he also served as the bouncer, from his looks and size. If my memory serves me right, there was a small stage toward the back and right side of the building. It was covered on the front and left side with some sort of chicken wire, which I assumed was to protect the band from flying objects. It sort of reminded me of the stage on the movie Roadhouse or Blues Brothers! Needless to say, this sort of got to us; we discussed whether or not we should even stay. Nevertheless, we overcame our fright and went ahead and set up. Well, surprisingly enough, the gig went along great. The crowd was not large, and everyone seemed to have a peaceful time! About halfway through the night, we took a second break and were glad to see that a businessman from Hardy dropped in and was setting at a table right next to the band stand. His name was Ervin and he was a chemical salesman who called on county offices, schools and hospitals between Hardy and Memphis. He also happened to be a good friend of Louis and I supposed that is how he knew we were playing there that night.

Out of nowhere, this young fellow walked up to me and started up a conversation. He said he enjoyed the music and told me his name. As I recall, he said it was Benny Bell. I said the guy was young, but he was probably a little older than me but not nearly as old as most of the others in the club that evening. He told me he sang and played the bass and wanted to know if he could sit in with us during the next session. I asked the other fellows, and they all agreed it was ok and so Bell started out with us when we resumed playing. Now our bass player, Louis, did not seem to care because he really liked to drink. He and his buddy, Ervin, had even captured the attention of a couple of local women, who, heretofore, had been sitting alone at the bar drinking.

So, as we completed that third session, Bell had remained playing and singing with us and old Louis and Ervin were pretty well into the company of their women friends by that time. As we sat down for a break, Louis came up to the three of us and asked if we could complete the last hour without him. He and Ervin were going to escort the two lovely ladies to Memphis, and they needed to get on the road.

Well, we figured it was ok, since everyone was pretty well plastered by that time, and no one would notice or care if the band was absent a bass man. It was during this time when we all lost track of our buddy Benny Bell and, truly, I don't recall any of us ever giving it a thought.

Before he left with Ervin, Louis asked that we pack his bass and amp up and take it back with us and we agreed. After the last session ended, Carol Ray collected the pay from the bartender, and we began to pack up to leave. Bob and his girlfriend, Sandy, had already left, leaving Carol Ray and myself to pack up all the gear for the trip back to Hardy. I am not sure which one of us picked up Louis' bass, but I do know the case was sitting on the back of the stage closed and locked, so I am sure we both assumed the guitar was inside. Now this being a brand-new bass and case, we had no idea of how much it weighed so when it was loaded up; we had no reason to think the instrument was not intact.

As you well know, it is usually pretty late when you leave a gig and that was the case with us; plus, we had a long way to drive before the night was over. When we got back to Hardy we went to Carol Ray's house, where we always kept the equipment and usually held our practice sessions. Our house was on the street right behind his and so I helped him unload the equipment to the back bedroom of their house before going home. I would guess it was nearing 2 a.m. when I finally got home.

A few days went by and we decided to have a practice at Carol Ray's house on Friday evening before we did a show at the Strawberry High School on that coming Saturday. Well, me and Bob had arrived a little early and were setting up the drums and hooking up the guitar amps along with Carol Ray. Then, about ten minutes after we had hooked up, Jay, who was leaving school, called to say he would be late and asked if he could use Louis' bass, to save him time from having to drive out to his house in Cherokee Village to get his own equipment. Carol Ray told him Louis' guitar and amp were still in the bedroom and he knew Louis would not care if Jay used them. So, Louis' equipment remained in the bedroom, untouched since we loaded it up at the C&R a few nights earlier.

About that time, Louis drove up and came into the dining room where we were hooking up for the practice. He said he had a gig that night with his regular band in West Plains and had come to pick up his equipment. Carol Ray said OK and told him it was still in the back bedroom, where we had left it that night. Louis, being in a bit of a hurry rushed back to the bedroom and came out with the guitar case in one hand and the bass amp in the other. He said, "Boys where is my guitar?" Well, it puzzled me, and I could tell it puzzled Bob too. As for Carol Ray, knowing he was somewhat of a prankster, I figured he hid the guitar to trick Louis, knowing he was in a hurry to leave. Ole Louis cursed a bit and said, "Come on, give me the guitar. I have to be on the road now, so I won't be late."

I believe, at first, we all thought Carol Ray was still pulling his leg and would soon reveal where the guitar was. But soon it was apparent, he was not joking. He turned to me and asked if I had seen the guitar and I strongly expressed that the last time I saw it was when we were at the C&R Club and that guy who sat in had set it down at the back of the stage when we finished the session. I, like Carol Ray, had assumed it was in the closed case, when we packed up to leave the club that night.

Apparently, and as a great shock to us all, the guitar had not been in the case when we left Trumann that night. So, I reminded the guys about the fellow who had sat in with us and used that bass guitar and we all guessed that, somehow, he was the culprit in the missing instrument story.

Some weeks went by before there was any further word on the missing bass. I know Louis had gone on and purchased another instrument and we had all just about forgotten about the loss of the original guitar. As fate had it, Louis had a brother who operated a barber shop on Main Street in Batesville. This shop was only a few stores down the street from the local music store. One day, Lester, who was a musician and brother to Louis, walked into that music store, not looking for anything in particular but some guitar strings. He noticed a very expensive Fender bass guitar hanging on the shelf, which was apparently not new, but closely resembled the one his brother had bought several weeks earlier. Knowing about his brother's missing instrument, he told the store manager about it and asked if he could take down the serial number from it, which the store owner agreed to. The store owner told Lester he had recently bought the guitar from a young man who came by and said he was leaving town and needed to sell his bass.

Well, Lester came up to Ash Flat that afternoon to tell his brother what he had found in Batesville and, lucky for him, Louis still had the sales papers and factory papers which contained the serial number of his instrument. They matched! Afterward, with the help of the County Sheriff, they were able to recover the guitar from the shop and the shop owner did recall that the guy who sold him that bass was indeed a Mr. Charley Bell.

ELVIS IN BATESVILLE

Batesville is located on the White River in the Ozarks. Every summer the Chamber of Commerce hosted a festival, the White River Water Carnival. Part of the excellence of the fest has been the music concerts that take place just next to the spillway of the river's landing. One year they booked Elvis.

For a time (and many years later), I lived and worked in Batesville. One day I dropped by the apartment of a friend, Dude, for a visit. We finally got around to the upcoming fest.

Dude's girlfriend at that time was Kellyanne. The more beer she chugged, the more animated she became about the upcoming River Fest, what a great time will be had. She told us that her father was in the Chamber of Commerce and was the chairman of the committee to pick the entertainment. The band that was booked this year was Mitch Ryder and the Detroit Wheels. She went on that in years past some really big stars had played the White River Water Festival, that even Elvis had; and that he had gotten into a fight that night and was thrown into jail. Kellyanne was starting to get outlandish, and

I was getting more and more skeptical.

I told her that I didn't believe what she had just said. In a huff, she said, "Well then, go research it yourself," which I did. I talked to several people who I thought were probably in town at the time. Most remembered it very well. I went to the city library to see what I could find in the old newspaper. Indeed, I found the article announcing the upcoming fest. The newspaper announced the Duke of Paduca as the main act. Down at the end, the bill announced, "and the Elvis Presley Band." Hard to imagine that this was a time that people were not familiar with that name. Elvis had a couple of regional hits at the time. It was 1952 and he was about to break out in a big way. Along with Elvis (according to the newspaper) was Scotty Moore on guitar. Tom Parker had negotiated two sets with Elvis and the Chamber of Commerce.

Elvis would go on first. Just imagine the stress of following big E. The Duke of Paducah (AKA Francis Ford) was a star too and counted many fans. He was a big-time DJ at WLS in Chicago. Banjo player.

Soon, 2 p.m. rolled around and Elvis took the stage. He really kicked it out. Everyone crowded around; no one had ever seen anything like this. Elvis did his hip shaking thing.

Of course, all the older crowd hated it and the young crowd was in a frenzy. When the ten-song set was over, the Chamber called for an emergency meeting to talk things over. What they agreed on was that there was to be no evening set for Elvis.

They summoned Tom Parker and gave him the news. He called around and found a gig. A band was needed for a party in the small town of Raven's Den about fifty miles to the east. It was there that Elvis got in a fight with one of the locals. Elvis was called before the sheriff and was thrown in jail.

Years later it happened that I was driving down that same stretch of highway late at night. It was the three of us; myself,

Debbie and her friend Judy. We talked to pass the time. Judy is a wonderful person with an expanded personality. I told her my theory that everyone has an Elvis story. Judy did not voice an opinion.

I needed gas, so I stopped at the Raven's Den Convenience Store. I was very surprised at what I saw. In spite of the late hour, the store was full of people. We were standing in the check-out line when Judy declared "Attention, may I have your attention please? My friend here tells me that Elvis came here once. Is there anyone here that knows anything about that?" Most of the people held up their hand. Judy and I had a great time visiting with everyone that night.

Several people recalled that Elvis went to a party after the gig. A young drunk goaded him into a fight. That's when he was jailed.

MARK SALLINGS, 1992

"All the mighty oaks are falling like victims of the cross-cut saw."

Many of us lost a good friend. The blues scene in the Natural State will never be the same since Mark Sallings left the building. He will certainly be missed.

It is impossible to reflect on the music of Mark Sallings and the Famous Unknowns without considering the continual compelling influence that the harmonica had on Mark's life. He was arguably one of the best blues harp players on the planet. He studied it on a fundamental level, taught it at Memphis State University and even won a Grammy for his mastery of this versatile blues machine. Mark was able to explain the mathematical secrets of the harp, as well as the raw emotional impact it has held over many generations, from the Delta cotton patches to the sophisticated salons of New York City.

The harmonica was at the center of one of Mark's first memories. Among his early recollections was sitting on the knee of Fayetteville patron saint, Ronnie Hawkins, as Hawkins played the harp and courted Mark's aunt, Joy Sue, while they babysat at Mark's grandmother's home in Combs while his mother swam in the White River. Hawkins' early tutoring started the boy on a life-long road of playing his brand of the blues for many diverse audiences.

Mark recalled Benny Goodman as another influence. Before Goodman became a big band star, his hot combo included such notables as Count Bassey and Lionel Hampton. His father's old records planted in Mark a blue note that was pulled through Goodman's clarinet.

At age ten, Mark played his first song in public (*Saint Louis Blues*). In the seventh grade he was invited to join a musical group of older boys in a local talent contest. He had been playing the sax for two weeks. His group won the contest. That was his start in show business.

Like most of the truly authentic blues players, Mark's epiphany came in a Delta cotton field, or rather, in his attempts to escape one. At age sixteen, he found that he could make more money chopping saxophone in the local bars than in working the fields. At that point, he quit chopping cotton in the hot and dusty patches of Woodruff County and put down his hoe for good.

While playing at the original Porky's Rooftop and the other beer joints around Newport, he was exposed to the more primal blues strains of Howlin' Wolf and Lightin' Hopkins. That revelation made the connection that seemed to explain to him the genius of the more refined chops of Goodman and Company. One can still hear both perspectives in Mark's recordings.

Later, Mark left college to embark on a lifetime odyssey of

making music his full-time profession. Before long he was a serious player in the Memphis sphere of influence. He never looked back but gave his concentrated focus to playing the Blues in a four-piece road band.

Mark Sallings and the Famous Unknowns released four record albums: *Up Close and Personal* (1992), *Let it Be Known* (1995), *Talking to Myself* (1998) and the prophetic *Temporary Life* (2008). Mark's abilities on the harp really had to be seen and heard to be appreciated Blues aficionados who had a chance to catch him in concert were indeed lucky to hear his blues from both sides.

The last time I saw Mark, he was scheduling a gig in Fayetteville, LJ's on College Avenue. Mark asked me to write a piece for the local newspaper, and I wanted to interview him for it. I met Mark for breakfast one beautiful spring morning at the Bowling Alley Café. What a shame that in a few days, Mark would be taken from us in a head-on collision. But on that day, that perfect spring day, we talked over a delicious breakfast and made plans for the future.

I asked about his latest album, *Temporary Life*. "Temporary life, what does that mean? Why would you name your album that?"

He looked very somber and said, "Just take a look around." He made a sweeping motion with his arm. "It's all an illusion, just an illusion. We are looking though a veil at moving shadows. But the veil will be dropped, and the stone will be rolled away."

I looked around in the café. All around us, people scarfing down pancakes and such. I have got to say that humans are not so beautiful when we feed. I think I understand what he was trying to tell me.

A few days after our conversation, I got the news. Mark, from all your friends, thank you so much for the things you did, and for the righteous blues you gave us.

Mark approached the harmonica seriously, not as a novelty; and from a horn player's point of view. I asked him to explain to me his technique.

Mark told me, "If you have an A harmonica, it is designed to be played in that key, all of the notes of the A major scale are in it. If you blow on the harp, you will get an evenly set up chord in that key. The notes of the draw side will be the five-chord of what is stamped on the harmonica. So, if you have an A harmonica and draw on the bottom end of it, you get a B chord. But after the first four holes, the way the cross-chord (the E) is set up, inherently, you have a ninth chord.

"The harp is set up to play songs like *Oh Suzanna*, but when the Blues players started looking for a sound to get out of it, they realized that there is a big, sweet sounding ninth chord that will come out of this thing too. So, they started picking around trying to find the notes that would allow them to play the Blues melodies based on that chord, instead of the major chord it was meant to be played in.

"The problem is that there are some notes that are not there, so you work around them, and you bend notes that can be bent to try to achieve the notes that are not there. For instance, there is no Major Seventh in the middle of a harmonica, but you can make one on the two-hole, drawing. You can bend it a half step down and you get a Major Seventh. On the top end (on hole nine), you can bend the blow note a half step down and you have a Major Seventh.

"What I figured out is that there is one place where you can make part of the five cords for E (in hole four, drawing), which would be a B. I use that, and it is one of the things that seems to baffle people."

Mark, from all the friends you left behind, we miss you very much.

DEBBIE IN JAMAICA

Debbie stands in front of the Farmers Market in downtown Montego Bay, Jamaica while Coy is on the Hip Strip. In Jamaica, you will find abject poverty beside the opulence of the moneyed class. Anyone who walks up to you will likely try to scam you. The State Department has lately issued a severe warning for Montego Bay and for the Hip Strip in particular. Think about it if you are interested in a Jamaican holiday. Then think twice. What a shame.

PATOIS - OCHO RIOS

The patois dialect is an enduring one. Jamaicans speak it, in part, to be able to communicate with each other, but not be understood by the slave masters. These days, they speak it around tourists for the same reason.

I was in Ocho Rios, sitting at the bar of the Hyacinthe Lounge having a Red Stripe. The two others at the bar were the bar maid and another customer. He was trying to get friendly with her. He told her (in patois), "You better go home and wash your little punny because I'm going to lick you up and lick you down." She replied (again in patois), "You would have to lick me because your wood is dead." She turned to me and said (this time in Queen's English), "It's a good thing you can't understand what we are saying."

TONY

"Hey mon, don't you recognize me?" That's a basic come-on for any higgler in downtown Montego Bay. I've heard it several times. "I'm Tony, I carried your bags for you at the airport. Tony seemed to appear from out of nowhere next to the bridge by Sam Sharp Square. "Big music tonight!" he said. "Bonti Killa, Beany Man; big music tonight at Pier One!"

"Catch you later, Tony." I turned and walked in the opposite direction, toward my destination of the Health Unit on Creek Street. But Tony persisted as he walked along beside me.

"No mon wait, it's not that easy. You've got to give me some money."

"For what? I was just walking down the street; I didn't ask you for anything."

"But I've got to have some money."

"Sorry," I said.

"Listen, mon, this is serious." As Tony spoke, he moved closer to my face, "You've got to give me some money. I've got to have some money." He pointed off into the distance. "Me and my friend, we run this whole area. Nobody passes through here without giving us money."

"Sorry," I repeated, still walking. He didn't give up. "You must give me money now or your blood will flow."

"What?" I couldn't believe what I just heard him say. It took a couple of seconds for it all to sink in. "Give me money now or your blood will flow." He said it again slowly and carefully. This time he enunciated each syllable so that I would be sure to fully understand what he said. "Why are you hassling me? I didn't hassle you. What did I do to you?"

He had a very serious look on his face. "So now you want me to understand. Well, understand this." To ensure my attention he gave me a swift head-butt right between the eyes.

It worked. He had my full attention right away. "If you don't give me money right now, your blood will flow. Do you understand what I am saying? This is no joke." No one seemed to have noticed what had just happened; or if they did, they did not react. They just passed us by.

I was stunned by the unexpected head-butt and shook my stinging head to clear the fog. "I've been to Jamaica many times, and no one has ever hassled me. Now you are going to be the first?"

"Oh," he said. "You say you gave been to Jamacia before? Let me look at your face." Tony examined my face closely, then looked me up and down. "Yes, you have the right look. Just forget it mon, pass on through."

JOHNNY CASH IN JAMAICA

Drunk History is a funny TV show, at least for the first couple of times you watch. I saw an episode recently about Kris Kristofferson and his efforts to come to Nashville and write hit songs. Kris was fixated on Johnny Cash and on convincing Johnny to record some of his tunes. Needless to say, Kris could never work his way through the layers of yes-men to get an audience with Johnny. He went to the extreme of flying a Huey helicopter to Johnny's house and landing it on his front lawn.

Johnny came running out to see about the commotion and shook hands with Kristofferson.

This story was certainly of interest to me, as I can somewhat relate to the situation (without the Huey part). But personally, I found it very easy to drive right up to the door and meet both Johnny and June.

Johnny Cash is a national hero in Jamaica. He first went to the island on invitation from John Rollins. In 1977, Rollins, a successful American entrepreneur, purchased Rose Hall Plantation, a few miles outside Montego Bay. Once he had purchased it, he sat about spending much of his sizable fortune in the total restoration of the now elegant villa.

He offered Johnny an adjoining tract of land which became Cinnamon Hill. Every year Johnny and his family spent the holidays there. The Jamaicans accepted the family into their embrace. The Cashes did good works in Jamaica, contributing to orphanages and underwriting health and educational initiatives.

A pivotal event occurred at Cinnamon Hill one night when the villa was invaded by three men armed with guns and knives. They were intent on robbing Johnny. The family was bound and threatened. Luckily, no one was hurt. The men took what they wanted and left.

Justice was swift. The men who perpetrated the robbery were quickly arrested. Jamaica is a relatively small island (about the same area as Arkansas). Nothing happens there without a lot of people knowing the particulars. During the trial, Johnny came to every court session.

The men were found guilty. On the day of sentencing, Johnny asked to address the court. He listed for the judge several extenuating circumstances for the crime and plead for mercy for the men. That is how Johnny Cash became a national hero in Jamaica.

I arrived in Montego Bay one Saturday afternoon. One of the first things I did was to buy a *Jamaica Gleaner*. On the front page was a story about Johnny and June arriving on the island for the holiday season. They had given a performance at Rose Hall Great House (this happened while I was enroute. Darn it, missed it). What a shame to miss one of the last performances of such legends. I tore out the news article, put it in my shirt pocket and walked on down to the Hip Strip.

Down on the street there are always lots of robot taxis. These are drivers who are not licensed by the government to provide that service. But no one complains. These are people who have somehow been able to lease or buy an automobile and do business without government sanction.

A driver called out to me, "Do you need a good driver mon; want a taxi?"

I walked over and pulled out the newspaper article and asked, "Do you know where Johnny lives?"

He looked at the article and said: "Yes mon, I know exactly where he lives."

I asked, "How far is it from here?"

"Not much mon, fifteen miles or so."

I said, "Let's go."

Life is good.

My driver was Jah David and he asked me all the standard questions as we proceeded down the road: "Your first time in Jamaica? How long will you be staying? Care for a smoke?" And finally, he got around to Johnny.

"Do you know Johnny; does he know you are coming?" Jah David switched to Patios when he encountered his brethren along the way. It can be very interesting to be around Jamaicans when they assume you cannot understand their dialect; but that is another story.

We rolled up to Cinnamon Hill, a beautiful estate, exotic

plants, lawn like a carpet. The whole area was immaculate. A stern-faced guard with a .38 Smith and Wesson paced the lawn.

Jah David asked, "Should I wait for you?"

"No, I don't know how long I will be. We can settle-up now."

I walked up to the gate and looked toward the pool (about thirty feet to the west). There sat Johnny and June. They looked just like one another. They both had big bouffants of silver-gray hair combed up and over (we have a saying back home: died, fried and laid to the side). They wore identical gym suits made of material with a metallic look.

"May I help you?" The guard approached me, his hand resting on the .38.

"I just want to say hello to Johnny. We are both from the same place in Arkansas." I handed him my business card from the University of Arkansas. The guard examined the card with a puzzled expression.

"Johnny is having breakfast now and cannot be disturbed."

"I don't want to disturb Johnny I just wanted to say hello from Arkansas."

Meanwhile, Johnny craned his neck to identify the sources of voices so early in the morning.

"Wait here." He walked over to Johnny and handed him the card. Johnny sighed and motioned for me to come over to poolside. Johnny and June were very gracious; they offered me some Blue Mountain coffee. We talked about Poinsette County. Johnny reminisced about making music at the Cotton Club and the C&R down on Highway 63.

After a bit, Johnny said, "Well, we have a few things to do this morning, but it's always good to visit with a fellow Arkie. Do you have a way back to town?"

"Yes, I can get back with no problem. Thank you very much, y'all have a fine day." And it was indeed a brilliant morning.

I walked about a half mile down the long driveway, climbed a tall fence, ran across the fairway of a golf course (risky business), back over the fence and I was on the highway. Flag a ride and I am speeding west back toward MoBay. Not long after that and back in Arkansas, I watched the *Walk the Line* movie. It spends a good deal of time on Dyess, Arkansas and the many occurrences there that shaped Johnny's life.

June died not long after I met them; then, it was not very long until Johnny left the building too. And so will we all. Ultimately, we are all dead men.

OCIE FISHER: THE GENUINE ARTICLE

I knew Rich from my work, but I didn't know that he was such a skilled blues player with the harmonica. I saw Rich the night we opened for Taj Mahal. I told him that I was looking for a gig. He asked me, "What kind of music do you play?" I told him, "Both kinds, Blues and Rhythm and Blues." He laughed and told me to come by tomorrow night and bring a rig.

Ocie Fisher was there along with some other players (most of them I already knew). For a relative newcomer Ocie really set Fayetteville on its ear. That's because she is indeed the real thing, the genuine article. Her contribution to the blues scene became so dramatic that she was awarded the coveted Best Female Vocalist by the NAMA Music Awards. Watch her perform and you will understand why the crowds cheer Ocie on with such enthusiasm. It's because she delivers the goods with a style and a flare that makes each blues standard her very own anthem.

We started to rehearse on a regular basis and before long it became evident that Ocie had assembled Fayetteville's top blues men and had drilled their chops until they had become a solid unit, speaking with one deep voice that renders roots music dried, fried and laid to the side.

It is incredible to reflect upon how many singing awards Ocie earned in a short period of time. I stopped counting at nine. The band won Best Blues Band five consecutive years and was inducted (some may say indicted) into the NAMA Hall of Fame. To cap it all off, Hipp Doggs recorded and released Best Album of the Year: *Bad Dog Blues*.

Ocie Fisher certainly does have an affinity for Blues music. She explains that "the Blues is something deep down that everyone can feel. Everybody has been through hard times. So just sitting back and listening to something soulful just touches you. It is basically spiritual too. It is special because these are true songs."

This affinity for the music and for the audience shows in Ocie's live performances. She is known for leaving the stage to merge with fans when she sings. "I like to get close to the people. They like to see me coming. They get all excited. They run and flock around and everyone wants to sing. They are all excited to sing with me. I have to keep a firm grip on the microphone. The Hipp Doggs got me a wireless microphone so that I can get out in front with the audience and run around."

"I want our group to be able to do more than just Blues songs. We are all interested in Gospel. I want to be able to play in churches too."

LUDA

In the past, it was my ritual every Sunday morning for newspaper and coffee. On one Sunday I spied an ad in the paper asking and recruiting those interested in forming a jazz combo. The writer was looking for someone to play sax or bass fiddle. I went to and passed an audition and joined with Luda and her husband Tom in a twenty-eight year run. Dave, one of my friends from other bands, took over drumming chores. Looking back on our jazz stint, I feel pride and satisfaction.

My favorite gig was totally unplugged and acoustic; a threesome: Dave on drums, Luda on baby grand, me on double bass. Another time we were invited to play at the haunted Crescent Hotel in Eureka Springs at a statewide training event. The place was packed and there was good food, good drinks but no ghosts. Thanks, Luda, for all the good times!

DRIFTWOOD

Several years ago, I had the great pleasure of working for the Area Agency on Aging. One of my duties was to design an employment program, finding jobs for people over age fifty-five. I was working Stone County and got word that a local dinner theater would be needing to hire for the upcoming season.

I did some research and found that the business was owned by Jimmy Driftwood, a name that sounded vaguely familiar to me. I made an appointment to speak with him about our program. I did more research and was surprised to find out about his background in songwriting.

I was anxious to meet him. I made the trip to Timbo, near Mountain View (about ten miles to the northwest). Take Highway 66. It's a beautiful drive. I got to my appointment early, so I walked around a bit, then went in. The dinner theater is a rustic approach to decorating with split oak handmade furniture. The walls are paneled with red oak two by tens. Each table had a red tablecloth. It was a homey atmosphere. The staff was busy getting ready for a big night.

The door opened and in stepped Jimmy Driftwood carrying a peculiar looking instrument. After introductions we talked about what we could accomplish. He told me that he was indeed very interested. I asked Driftwood if he would consider allowing me to interview him for an article in our newsletter. He said yes and we set an appointment for the following week.

The week rolled by and once again I found myself in Timbo. This time I was sitting down to interview a living legend in the music industry. Here is what transpired:

CH: Mr. Driftwood, the last time I saw you, you were carrying a very unusual instrument. Could you tell me a little about it?

Driftwood: My family was always poor. We had no disposable income whatsoever. When I was a young boy, I got the idea that I had to have a guitar. I mean I really had to have one. I told my granddad about it. He explained to me that we would have to use what was at hand to make a guitar. We got two slats from under his mattress and found several other things at home we could convert. We were stumped when we got to strings. Finally, we decided to use strands of fencing. I have played that guitar for thirty years and recorded two albums with it.

CH: How many songs have you written?

Driftwood: My manager tells me that we have copywritten seven thousand songs.

CH: Do you remember writing your first song?

Driftwood: Yes, I wrote my first song when I was around eight. I wrote a song about my dog, Bullet.

CH: For all the aspiring song writers that might read this article, how do you write a song?

Driftwood: As far as my songs are concerned, I don't even try to write unless I have something important to say to someone. The song condenses around that important something. Many times, these songs come from my dreams. Otherwise, my advice to aspiring songwriters: keep a journal. During my teaching years, I wrote songs to use as teaching aids, That's where *Battle of New Orleans* came from, to help the students with dates and such.

CH: You have received so many accolades and awards, do you recall any special ones?

Driftwood: One great time in my life I recall so well was when I was invited to play at Carnegie Hall. Not so bad for a sharecropper's son. I guess most notable commercially would be winning the Grammy award for Song of the Year. My stock started going up at that point. Just at that time, I was voted into the County Music Hall of Fame in Nashville, Tennessee.

CH: Do you continue to write and record?

Driftwood: I really can't see a point in my life when I wouldn't want to write. It is catharsis. I have a recording studio in my basement that I use sometimes when friends come over to jam. I haven't been on tour in years. I prefer to stay near the ole wood stove. I can tell you for a certainty that I like the lifestyle of the Ozarks much more than the one of Hollywood.

AN INTERVIEW WITH THE MYSTERIOUS JOHNNY DOUGH: MANY SECRETS REVEALED

For several months now, rumors have been flying around Fayetteville about Dr. Johnny Dough. Some say he made a small fortune in IPOs, then bailed out just in the nick of time. Others say he recently completed a PhD financed by the C.I.A. Some even say that he has been in the Witness Protection Program and lately decided to resurface. Well, whatever the truth turns out to be, one thing is certain: Dough's strong bass licks are solidly grounded in the blues. I was finally able to communicate directly with him to convince him to clandestinely meet me for this interview. My resolve was to try to get to the bottom of all the talk around town and to find out the truth about the mysterious Dr. Dough.

CH: Johnny, you have been somewhat successful at creating a truly mysterious persona. Why is Johnny Dough so darned mysterious?

JD: I'm not all that mysterious. I'm just a person who likes the quiet, simple life. I don't believe in a lot of hoopla.

CH: But you have agreed to an interview in this very popular magazine. That's lots of hoopla, isn't it?

JD: Susan Porter talked me into it. Besides, I'm always very glad to have a nice conversation with such pleasant company.

CH: How did you get the blues?

JD: I got the blues just like everyone else did. I got them in the cotton field.

CH: The cotton field?

JD: The cotton field will certainly give you the blues. You know, that's where the blues all got started. It was called field hollerin'. The function of the blues has always been catharsis.

Folks would be out in the field in the hot sun chopping weeds. You just can't help it; you finally have to wail out loud, "Please Lord, anything but this. Please just get me outta here!" I did a fair amount of field hollerin' myself.

CH: How long have you been playing the bass guitar?

JD: I started playing the bass a long time ago. My friend, James, in high school had a band. He played the bass; and his brother, David, played the six string. James wanted to start playing rhythm in the band so he needed someone for bass. He asked me did I think that I could play one and I said yes, although I didn't even know what a bass was then. I just knew that I wanted to rock. He had an old Danelectro Longhorn bass guitar, now a collector's item. After school we would go to his house and he would show me this and that. I saved my money and one day we ditched school and went to Beale Street in Memphis. At that time, the south side of Beale was lined with musty old pawnshops, and we would spend all day crawling through those shops looking at guitars instead of going to trigonometry class. So, that day I bought a bass guitar for $16, a microphone for $18, and I was in the entertainment business. James had purchased a Sears Silvertone amplifier on credit, and we plugged three guitars and a mic all into that one amp.

CH: Do you still have that first guitar?

JD: No. A few weeks after buying it, I graduated to an old Fender and I sold the first one.

CH: What bass guitar do you use now?

JD: I have three basses now, but my favorite is a Fender Precision. It's a 1998 American Standard model, one of the last American Standards to be made, I think. It's a very sweet guitar. The amplifier that I use is an Ampeg that I got from Ben Jack. The head has 350 watts of power. I use two cabinets, one with a fifteen-inch speaker, the other with two ten-inch speakers. I am surprised over and over again by how much punch that amp has. So, I am very satisfied with the particular rig that I'm playing right now. I think it's the best rig in town.

CH: How would you characterize your style of playing?

JD: I always liked Blues and Rhythm and Blues and tried to play like I heard Duck Dunn play. I was heavily influenced by what was happening in Memphis. We would listen to WDIA, "50,000 watts of good will." Rufus Thomas always played some good records. Anyway, that's the music I played while I was coming up; Otis Redding, Al Green, Sam and Dave. That's the music I still like to play and listen to.

My theory is to keep it simple and keep a good bottom line going. Bass players generally go through several stages along the way. But finally, a good player will settle down, evolve away from the esoteric stuff and start hitting with the precision of pistons in a V-8 engine.

CH: Did you get to meet any of those Memphis players?

JD: I got to meet a few people. Charlie Rich borrowed my amp to play a gig in Jonesboro. Of course, that was when he was noteworthy but obscure, but he had just cut *Lonely Weekend.* Remember Sam the Sham? During high school I worked at the local radio station, KTMN. Sam the Sham would periodically come by to plug his latest record. He was a real hoot. It wasn't too long until Sam had the number one song on Billboard, had sold eight million copies of *Wooly Bully*, and was opening for the Beatles. About that same time, Jerry Jay recorded the old Fats Domino song *Hello Josephine* for Hi Records in Memphis. Everybody was sure surprised when that song got to be number sixteen in the nation almost overnight. I played the bass for Jerry several times around the Missouri Bootheel in some of the real rough roadhouses they had over there; slug your way in and slug your way out.

CH: Did you do any recording in Memphis?

JD: I did some recording at the Sonic Studio on Madison

Street. Roland James owned the studio. Roland was the piano player for Sam Phillips at Sun Studio for many years. Most of the famous Sun tunes have Roland playing on them. He later built his own studio around the corner from Sun. He had a very funky studio but was able to get a great sound out of those old half-track Wollensak machines. The place was very competitive. Most anyone who happened to be in the studio at any particular time was a superb musician. When the reels started to roll, the heat was on. Anyway, one song we recorded and got pressed into a 45 record was *Priscilla.* We finally got it put on the jukebox and just about wore it out, playing it over and over.

CH: How did you end up in Fayetteville?

JD: Seventeen years ago, I decided to go back to school. I came to Fayetteville to study at the university. Also, there was a particular woman I wanted to be close to, a Carroll County girl.

CH: Tell me some of the details about the *Tommy* project. How did you get involved in it?

JD: It is just so great to be involved in *Tommy*; it is the fulfillment of a long-time dream. I saw The Who in Memphis in the late 60s; they did some of the songs from *Tommy*. It made a big impression on me at the time. I went out and bought the music and learned the charts. I had friends who liked the songs too; we would sit around and play them. But that was a long time ago, and it's difficult to find folks who are really familiar with the score. I always wanted to play the tunes, perhaps in a special set in a band, but I was never able to pull that off. Very few people want to invest all the time and effort in a project as specialized as that.

I got interested again a couple of years ago when John Entwistle played down on Dickson Street at Chester's. As soon as you walked in the door, there was a large glass jar full of cotton balls for fans to stuff in their ears. That kind of was the tip-off of what was to come. He played the very loudest that I had ever heard anyone play anywhere. It was funny. Entwistle told the audience that in every band he had played, people kept telling him to turn it down, turn it down. He said that this was his band and that he was going to turn up as loud as he wanted. Then he turned around and proceeded to turn his amp up to eleven and just wailed. He was incredibly loud, like two B52s taking off.

He played the two *Tommy* songs that he wrote: *Cousin Kevin* and *Fiddle About*; certainly not the best songs of the opera, but interesting. I'm glad that I got to see Entwistle that night, because in six short months he was deceased.

Anyway, I was excited to see that the University of Arkansas was presenting *Tommy*. I called Paul Summerlin (the music director) right away and arranged for an audition to play bass. For the audition we played the overture. I was excited when they hired me for the job. There were a lot of good players that auditioned. Later I asked Paul why he chose me for the gig. He said, "Of all those players, you are the only one that saw The Who in concert. You are the roots mon."

Paul's production is superb, first-rate, so much fun. I hope that everyone will turn out to see it. We'll do eight shows, so everyone should have the chance to see the opera. It's this year's big musical event.

CH: Is there a blues connection to *Tommy*? I always considered those songs to be pop.

JD: Not that there's anything wrong with pop songs, but yes there is a strong blues connection to *Tommy*. The very centerpiece of the opera is *Eyesight to the Blind*, the classic old blues tune written by Sonny Boy Williamson, an Arkie from Helena. Sonny Boy lived and died in obscurity and poverty, like most of the blues pioneers. The Broadway version of *Tommy* treats the song as the blues, even more so than the Who album does. [He lapses into the song, singing it with a blue note] "You talk about your woman, I wish you could see mine.... You talk about your woman, I wish you could see mine.... When she starts to lovin' she gives eyesight to the blind."

CH: You've come a long way in a short time. How did it feel to be voted Best Blues Band in the NAMA poll?

JD: Yes, it was sure an exhilaration to just be nominated in the same category with such great blues players as the likes of Michael Burks, much less to actually win the award. It was a very humbling and a joyous experience for me personally and for the band collectively. We really worked hard on the music. Fayetteville is a community where blues is very popular; people take it seriously. So, we all realize how important this award is, and will try to live up to everyone's high expectations.

CH: And then you opened for blues great, Taj Mahal. How was that experience?

JD: That was just great. I've been a Taj Mahal fan since 1969 when I bought one of his albums from a cut-out bin (*The Natch'l Blues*). It had so many great tunes on it: *She Took the Katy*, *Move on Up to the Country*, *Ain't That a Lot of Love*. It was really something to actually see him play and to meet him and talk to him after all this time. He has a handshake like a vice grip. His band was hot, and he put on a real show that night. And to answer your question, it was an exceptional experience.

CH: What are your present recording plans?

JD: I am indeed working on material for a new CD to be recorded soon. I have a friend in Nashville who is an excellent producer. He plans to come to town to help us on the project. We'll probably record at Junction Studio in Madison. We haven't worked out all the details, except to say we have found the right studio and the right engineer.

CH: Dr. Dough, I'm sure that you know that rumors have

been flying around about you and your past. Do you care to make any comments to our readers about these matters?

JD: Only to say that you really can't believe everything you see and hear, now, can you? But ashes to ashes. I say let's close the past box, put a lid on it and move on to the new business at hand.

CH: But there was a long period of time when you were somewhat underground. What was that all about?

JD: Yes, there was a long period of time that I was a hermit and lived at the end of the road, metaphorically and literally. I just needed some down time, that's all. There's something to be said for that. To be frank, I'm not so sure that I got that all out of my system. I liked it. I might return to that life someday soon. I still have ten acres at the end of the road in the Ozark National Forest. It would be the perfect place for a personal recording studio and compound that I have in mind to build someday.

CH: Do you have anything else to add?

JD: Yes, are you picking up this tab? Then I'll have another drink.

MOST IMPORTANT SONGS

Just for your own reference, I think that I should, at this time, list my most important songs so that you can see if we are on the same planet music-wise. I submit the county songs then the rock 'n' roll. These are not in a ranked list.

Country Songs

Walk the Line

Lonesome Fugitive

Great Speckled Bird

Coal Miner's Daughter

Crazy

It's Only Make Believe

Walking The Floor Over You

El Paso

He Stopped Loving Her Today

Your Cheating Heart

Rock Songs

Heart Break Hotel

Stairway to Heaven

Johnny B. Goode

I Wanna Hold Your Hand

Thriller

I Feel Good

Cocaine

Sad Eyed Lady of the Lowlands

Like a Rolling Stone

POST SCRIPT

PATOIS

Reading Jamaican patois is a very interesting exercise, even for someone who is unfamiliar with the dialect. One can sound it phonetically and listen for the English analog (for instance, Krismos becomes Christmas). Here is a good example of a short article written in patois. This article appeared in *The Observer*. The author describes a Black Power festival called Kwanzaa started in 1966 by an American professor. The article states that Kwanzaa lasts seven days. Each day is named with a word from the Swahili language. The author goes on to describe the seven days of the festival. The Roman festival of Saturn is referenced, along with Christmas on the plantation (plantieshan). The author closes by writing that the message advanced by Kwanzaa seems like the message that Jesus brought: Love others as you love yourself.

"Kwanzaa a wan neks festival ina disemba, ina 1966 wan Black Amerikan profesa man. Maulana Karenga, im kom op wid di aidiya fi staat op wan blak powa festival. Kwanzaa laas fi 7 die. It staat pan baksin die. Bai di wie, unu nuo wa mek dem kaal i "baksin die?" A chruu di rich piipl dem ina Ingglan yuuz tu baks op present fi gi dem worka pan dat de die.

Fi di 7 die a Kwanzaa, Karenga pik 7 difran wod fram Swahili, wan Afrikan langgwij, fi kansida. Fos dies, UMOJA. Yuuniti. Sekan die, KUJICHAGULIA. Dat miin wi ha fi du tingz fi wi self and no sidong a wiet pan ada piipl fi epl wi. Marcus Garvey uda lov dat. Neks die, UJIMA. Wi kom tugeda an elp wan anada ina di komyuuniti. Den yu av UJAMAA. Dis wan miin se wi fi bai an sel mongs wi was anada an bil op blak bizniz. Neks dies a NIA. Wi ha fi av a porpos ina laif. Den

KUUMAB. Wi ha fi nuo ou fi tek wi han ton fashin. Laas die a IMANL Fiet. Wi ha fi biliiv ina blak piipl.

Mi fiil se do huol a dem Disemba festval a selibriet di enin a di ier. Wi so glad fi si wi lass out wan neda ier, we ha fi du somting. Mi fiil sea it mek wi tek uol ier nait so siiryos. Penti piipl wa no bada wid Krismos chrai a ting fi nyuu ier. An wi mek huol hiip a pramis wi kyaan kip. Bot wi fiil gud Nyuu ier. Nyuu chaans fi chrai liv likl beta. Di Ruoman dem yuuz tu frii dem sliev fi Saturn festival. Gi dem a likl blai fi fyuu die. An boki maasa yuuz to dronk wi op fi Krismos pan di plantieshan. Mek wi fiil se wi frii. Ina dem ya taim wi ha fi frii op wi self fi chruu. Kwanzaa spirit ha fi lass fi di houl a dir ier. Siem laik di mesij wa Jesus did bring. Chrai love ada piipl laik ou yu lov yuself."

NOUS SOMMES DÉSOLÉ

We were on our way to the flea market at Clingancourt, on the outskirts of Paris. We took the Metro from Bir Hakeim to Denfert-Rochereau. Here we would catch the train to the north to Porte de Clingganancourt. The station at Denfert-Rochereau is a large hub where several Metro lines intersect. Rivers of people are leaving one train to catch another and to continue their journey. Being a hub makes Rochereau crowded and active. There are lots of people moving up and down stairways from one level to the next to get to their next train.

Debbie and I read the maps to find which platform for the Number Four to take us to the north. A thin woman stood on the platform with us. She bent over bundles, three bales of old newspaper, each bound together with a scarf, each bundle as big as a tire. We walked past her and I turned to see her face. She was dreadlocked and appeared destitute. Her clothes were old and somewhat dirty, shoes worn out long ago. But somehow, she radiated an air of grace and elegance, standing there on the platform. Debbie and I speculated about her and about her bundles. I thought that she was probably taking these bundles of newspaper to a recycling center. Debbie thought that the lady was homeless and carrying her bedroll; these bales were padding for sleeping in some niche somewhere.

We turned our attention to reading the signs and deciding where we could board Train Four. We would have to traverse several stairways to get to the correct platform. Down the hallway we went with the flow of the crowd. We came to the first stairway, and there standing before it was the dreadlocked lady. She laid her bundles on the floor and seemed to be steeling herself towards the chore of carrying them up several flights. I asked her in English if I could help her carry the load to the top of the stair, she nodded yes. I grabbed two of the bundles by the scarves that bound them and lifted. Both scarves instantly came off in my hands and both the bundles of newspapers unwound and went everywhere. This all happened in the middle of a fractious crowd of people, all anxious to get up the stairs and on their way.

"Nous somme désolés," Debbie told her. The three of us started reassembling the bundles in the middle of the hubbub. We handed her the newspapers and she reconstructed and tied the bales. A small silver spoon fell out of the middle of one of the bundles. It had been hidden deep in the very center of the bundle. It was a very old and fancy spoon, an unusual article to be thus hidden. Debbie picked up the spoon and handed it to its owner. The lady once again hid the object in the center of one of the bales. In a few minutes (and in spite of the rush of the crowd), we three were able to reassemble the load. Throughout the whole incident, the lady was very gracious to both of us. I knew better than to try to carry the bundles again, so we just left her there to struggle with them alone.

All the remainder of the day, Debbie and I were pensive. We both thought about the incident all afternoon, though we did not speak of it.

Later we made it back to our hotel on Quai de Grenelle and after a time, the dreadlock lady came up again in our conversation. Maybe we both felt a bit guilty about what had happened with the bundles, and in general about being wealthy enough to be able to come to France and enjoy ourselves when there were so many people pathetically struggling just to survive through another day.

"We could have given that lady some money for the trouble we caused, we could have given her fifty dollars, no big deal. Why didn't you give her some money?" Debbie asked me. I didn't think of it at the time. "Maybe we will see her again later at the Metro when we go out to dinner." I started computing in my mind the chance of ever really seeing this woman again; impossible - no way.

Dining in Paris takes some getting used to. The waiters will have their feelings hurt if you offer a tip; much different than in the States, isn't it? Not much for French cuisine, we like to go to the Parisian version of Tex-Mex, the Indiana Restaurant. The décor is a Frenchman's notion of the U.S.'s wild west. For mediocre food, the food is not half bad.

Once again, we boarded the Metro, heading north to Saint-Germain-des-Prés. The stop at Bienvenue is another hub and we again set out about deciphering the map and figuring out which train to catch.

There she stood by a coffee vending machine pulling its levers. I pointed her out to Debbie. Imagine the chances of seeing her again in a totally different part of town and in a crowded subway: one in two million. I walked over to her. She looked up and immediately recognized me. I said, "Comment va-t-il?" I reached out my hand with a twenty-euro note. She stared at it somewhat confused. "Pour moi?" She asked. "S'il vous plait" I answered. She smiled and took the note. We left her standing there looking at the euros and smiling. Debbie and I continued on our journey. We both felt so much better on our way to the Indiana.

THEORY

Why did I write this book? There are plenty of song writing books as it is. When I was planning for retirement, I concocted a plan to record four record albums and a book explaining the songs and the writing process.

Why is the theory so relevant to you the reader, both professionally and socially? First of all, I need to build a theory and list some hypotheses.

I believe theory is a speculation on how the world really works. What is then the connection between these items (theory and the hypothesis) as we see them today? We might look to Zen to help focus and to Prana Yoga for further help toward understanding.

Here are some good tools to put in our song writing toolboxes. I suggest that the reader takes a bit of time to research these techniques.

FREUD and JUNG

Jung and his fellow travelers look to Freud as children look to their father. In this case, we can find and use both of these theoretical leanings, Jung's mix of akashic records and Freud's universal sexuality. Music is a large component of the expression of our subconscious connections to the collective past that Jung told us about. The Greeks introduced us to the World of Forms where nothing is defined nor set in stone, a point in the structure of existence which is unknown.

One hypothesis might be that everyone has an Elvis story.

I make two predictions: Things are seldom as you thought they would be, so we will have to be careful when we get into that area. Having said that, I will find that many or most of the people I talk to do indeed have an Elvis story. I predict that I will be able to use meditation to help access lyrics from my subconscious mind.

Everywhere I go the peoples ask me how come I keep singing them sad, sad songs?

I tell them that sad songs is all that I know.

If I can help someone who is trying to write a song, that's all I need as payback.

PART II
LYRICS AS PROSE

BOGUS GOVERNMENT YO YO

Front cover: Debbie stands by a wall at the Farmer's Market in Montego Bay, Jamaica. A lady exits stage right.

Too bad things have changed so much in Jamaica. Can I get a witness? It's not just the Covid, though I will bet Covid is at the bottom of it all. The country has become unsafe, even in the all inclusives. If you are thinking about going to Jamaica, think twice. Maybe the crime wave in Jamaica will cool down with the passage of time. Stay tuned.

Back cover: While on the Hip Strip, Coy with a message to the ruling class, "The poor can't take no more."

Many of the songs on this album are old ones. Time was when I had some amount of angst in my life; and perhaps

to help me cope, I decided to write and record an album in Nashville.

Insert: Sunset at the Sea Wind; Neil Russell with Debbie.

Songs

Mighty White of You: Written for Ocie, but I never got the chance to play it for her.

Down at the Circle J: The Circle J is the C&R Club. Shannon Gage gave me the idea for this song.

Pumpin' Ethyl: Everyone's favorite.

My First Day in Chicago: Thank you Lectric Liz and Brother Dave Gardner.

The Lonesome Stranger: I am the lonesome stranger.

Russellville Blues: Shut it down now! ...safety concerns. Another reference to long distance call.

Beers in Heaven: It's about 50/50. Some say there is beer in Heaven, others say no. What do you say? Ubiquitous.

Priscilla: Recorded in Batesville.

Future Shock: Soon come.

No Slop for You: So, don't expect any.

Drafted by the Salvation Army: Based on Dave's holidays.

Can't Afford to Die: Another "Hard Shell" connection.

MIGHTY WHITE OF YOU

Key: D; Harp D/G

ride

First of all, you tell me you love me
Then you try to say that we're through
With sorrow just hanging above me
Darlin that's mighty white of you
My friends keep callin' long distance
To say you found somebody new
And men are just falling about you
Well, that's mighty white of you
Sed that's mighty white of you baby
Doin' all the things that you do
Knowin' that you're makin' me crazy
That's mighty white of you
Yea that's mighty white of you

ride

You layin' out every night Honey
Just knowin' you could never be true
Throwin' around all my money
That's mighty white of you
I'm gonna shoot one of us Baby
Right now I just don't know who
Won't help to make no fuss Baby
Sed that's mighty white of you
Well, that's mighty white of you Baby
To do all those things like you do
Doggin' me and making me crazy.
That's Barry White of you yea
That's Barry White of you.

I wrote this song for Ocie to record, but I never got a chance to show it to her. A couple of my friends have told me they thought it sounded racist, but no, it's not at all. It's just the opposite. It's tongue-in-cheek.

Much of the lyrics could be out of a Blues Brothers song: "I'm gonna shoot one of us baby, right now I just don't know who." I do like how the harp part of the song turned out. The song is played in D. The harp part (the best part of the song) is D over G. The tempo is 56. Notice that this song requires two harmonicas, a D over an E. See if you can spot where I change back and forth. This song reminds me of the blues song *Long Distance Call*; Lectric Liz introduced it to me. Thanks Liz. *Mighty White of You* is played in the key of D.

DOWN AT THE CIRCLE J

Key: G; Harp: C

Workin' hard in a dirty, cold Tyson
Tradin' all my time for a little pay
Just waitin' for that five o'clock bell to ring, son
I'm praying for the end of the day
But no one waits for me at home
She said she just couldn't stay
So, I'll go on down to the only family I know
Goin' down at the Circle J
Yes, happy hour, the saddest part of the day
And everything I had is gone away
A shot, a beer, then I'll listen to
That lonesome juke box play
"There stands the glass
It's my first one today."

ride
modulate
So, when I die
They'll dig me a hole
And there is where I'll stay
No one will come to see me then
Not even Bobby Crooze from the Circle J
And one day Lord when I am gone
She may come back this way
But she won't find me drinkin', thinkin'
And goin' down at the Circle J
Cause happy hour is the saddest part of the day
I just can't seem to drink these blues away any more
But I'll meet you down there again my friend
We'll drink my paycheck away
Cause happy hour is the saddest part of the day.
Yes, happy hour is the saddest time of the day.

I've seen many beer dives, and most seem pitiful in some way.

This story is an homage to Webb Pierce and his song *There Stands the Glass*. It is also about the C&R and the Cotton Club. The C&R and Cotton Club are Circle J. When I was young, I spent a considerable amount of time in both these beer joints. I saw some of the greatest rock 'n' roll acts of the time there. I regret that I never saw Elvis. He wanted to play these venues, but for some reason, Colonel Tom Parker would not allow it. Perhaps it was the fact that a stabbing or a gun fight in the parking lots of these establishments were not rare events.

Dirty, hot factory becomes dirty, cold factory.

Debbie's sister, Shannon, came up with the idea of "happy hour is the saddest time of the day."
Not even Bobby Crooze from Circle J.
The Circle J is the C&R Club.
Great steel guitar.
Modulate up a step.
They'll be sorry when I'm gone.
G chord, harp is C.

PUMPIN' ETHYL

I've got a brand-new gig on the gas station rig
I'm pumpin' Ethyl yea
It's not much money but I get a lot of honey
Pumpin' Ethyl, pumpin' Ethyl
When mornin' comes around you know
I can be found pumpin' Ethyl
I got a brand-new girl she's cutest in the world
Pumpin' Ethyl
She's not so smart but she stole my heart
Pumpin' Ethyl
And when the evening comes around, I can be found
Pumpin' Ethyl
Pumpin' Ethyl
It's premium tain ya'll
It's so easy to see I got a PhD
In Pumpin' Ethyl
I'm getting pretty good workin' under the hood and pumpin'
So many ways, so many days of Pumpin' Ethyl
Pump……

MY FIRST DAY IN CHICAGO

Key: E; Harp: A

Well, I ain't gonna work on my first day in Chicago
No, I ain't gonna work
Well, I ain't gonna work on my first day in Chicago no
I ain't gonna work
There's lots of things to see
Malcolm X's there on the TV
And I ain't gonna work
Well, my friend he left for Chicago
Gonna find some fortune and fame
Wrote me back sed I gotta come to Chicago
Cause back home it just ain't the same
He sent me the one-way fare to Chicago
And he wrote me about all I'd see
So much money right there in Chicago
He said that it just grows on the trees
Sweep it off the sidewalks of Chicago
Cause it's blowin' around just like the leaves
So, I ain't gonna work on my first day in Chicago,
No he ain't gonna work
I aint't gonna work on my first day
In this land of milk and honey
Lots of women, lots of money
So, I ain't gonna work, no not today no
Started that Greyhound on into Chicago
We pulled into the station there
Squinted in the bright sunlight of Chicago
All on my first day there
Walked outside the terminal building

And the very first thing I see
A crisp green one-hundred-dollar bill on the sidewalk
Just starin' right back at me
You know if I was still back home, I'd run over yonder
Scoop up all that dough
But today I just can't see me working
Gonna take it nice and slow
Cause I ain't gonna work on my first day in Chicago no
I ain't gonna work
Well, I finally made it here
I'll be a rich man in a year so I ain't gonna work
No no not today no
ride
Goin' down
Goin' down to see that Navy Pier
Goin' down
Goin' down to ride around on the L
Goin' down to see Ms. Sally
Listen to them play the blues
Dodging bullets right down on Michigan Avenue
fade

This song is certainly one of my favorites on the record album. I do remember the writing of it very well. I was in Negril, Jamaica. Jamaica is so conducive to writing songs. I was thinking of a song we did years ago in the Strait Jackets. The song was recorded by Jerry Jay over in the boot heel. *Haunted House* got to 18 on the billboard chart. I gigged with him a bit when he needed a spare.

The song is based on a Dave Gardner thing. So, that day in Jamaica, I was thinking about Brother Dave riffs that could morph into a song. I remembered the story about two young men who wanted something more than life in the cotton field. One young man goes north and writes his friend that up north money is so easy to get that it grows on the trees. His naive friend takes him literally.

When he gets to the promised land, he happens across a 100-dollar bill blowing down the sidewalk. He turns up his nose at it. Money is so easy, it can wait.

Thanks to Lectric Liz for introducing me to the bass line used in this song. It gives an interesting stop and go feel to the piece.

THE LONESOME STRANGER

Key: D; Harp: G

Well, he's the lonesome stranger
He's getting stranger and stranger
He's just a shadow that passes in the night
Hey prodigal drifter when will you find Goshen
When will you come stumbling into the light
No mother's arms will ever hold him
No woman will ever treat him right
And with no one there to console him
He's a strugglin' through the darkness and the night
And the lonesome stranger is armed and dangerous
And he's just about to lose his control
Hey, worn out wayfarer, is there a balm in Gilead
That can soothe the sin sick soul
ride
Yes, and he's tryin' so hard just to hold on
And he's tryin' not to let it show

That one day this prodigal grifter
Will know as he is known
And in the wee small hours of the midnight
Through some frost covered window he sees
His faraway family who once loved him
Long gone and it always will be
He's the lonesome stranger he's getting stranger and stranger
He's just a shadow that passes in the night
Hasta luego when will you find Goshen
When will you come stumblin' into the light

A few of these songs were written long ago. This is one of them. At the time I found myself in a most uncomfortable place in time. It seemed that most of my friends had turned their backs and loved ones did not seem so loving. I wrote the song about my situation.

I am the lonesome stranger.

Here is a connection with my mother. She was a "Hard Shell" Baptist. I think that means they did things the old-fashioned way.

The philosopher asks, "is there a balm in Gilead that can soothe the sin sick soul?"

The believer says, "there is a balm in Gilead that can soothe the sin sick soul!"

RUSSELLVILLE BLUES

Key: G7; Harp C

guitar intro

Gonna write a little letter, gonna send it to my congressman
All this nuclear pollution

Don't you think it's just a little out of hand
Fukushima exploded and there wasn't nothing left but sand –
radioactive sand
Started out so great yea and they told us it was grand
Lots of cheap energy
They all had it planned
But what will we do when they have ruined all our land
Roll over Einstein
Roll over Einstein
Roll it on over Einstein
Roll over Einstein
Roll over Einstein
And dig to these Russellville Blues
ride
Tell me, who can remember the "atomic empire"
And the meltdown back in seventy-nine.
The genie betrayed us
Turned to try and slay us
Left his footprints in the sands of our time
Mother Earth is calling long distance
And she's trying to get us on the line
Well early in the mornin' there's a siren a warnin'
About an H bomb tickin' so near
Hey hey Obama don't give us psychodrama.
Shut it down, get it outta here
Let's go to Russellville and kick their ass outta there.
Roll over Einstein
Roll over Einstein
Roll over Einstein
Roll over Einstein
Roll over Einstein

And dig to these Russellville Blues.

I have been in an atomic reactor three times. All the way to the fuel rods and to the spot where the atomic reaction takes place. Way back when, the University of Arkansas partnered with the Japanese government to build an experimental breeder reactor. A breeder reactor is designed to produce fuel rods for use at other sites. This particular project ran successfully for some years. But one day it came to an end. The Japanese just went home and left the reactor sitting empty for the university to deal with.

I went into the core area, the holy of holies. Underneath the spot where the core once hung is located a four-foot-tall cone. If the core started to melt down, it would land on the cone. This would separate the molted gob of plasma into several globs and would thus be easier to deal with.

The site, (a community called Hog Eye — I'm not kidding) sat dormant for years. Everyone knew that someday this reactor would have to be dealt with, but they kicked it down the road. From time to time unusual materials would be salvaged from the Hog Eye site (for instance, very thick glass panes). The Physical Plant's final solution became filling the entire unit with 7,000 pounds of concrete. I know of at least three more hazardous sites both on and off the campus, but that is another story for another day.

At Russellville is an atomic reactor that is designed to produce electricity. Relative to the other one hundred reactors in the United States, the Russellville reactor is one of the oldest. These reactors are ranked safety-wise. Russellville ranked 100th (in other words, THE WORST). There have been two deaths during the operations at the plant.

Russellville Blues is an old song that has stayed with me for years, decades. Time to shut it down, just like the one at Hog Eye.

This is definitely a Chuck Berry song, except roll over Einstein, not roll over Beethoven. He already rolled over. Bottom line: LET'S GO TO RUSSELLVILLE, LET'S KICK THEIR ASS OUTTA THERE.

BEERS IN HEAVEN

Key: A min; Harp: D

short intro

Hey, somebody told me
There'd be no beer up in heaven
That everybody gotta drink it all
Right here and now
No, no keno, no throwin' lucky seven
No million-dollar lotto
Like I always planned to win
Soon as my bad luck changes
And my praying starts kickin' in

ride

Hey somebody told me
There'd be no kush up in heaven
That everybody gotta just settle for shake
No late night taboos
No worn-out yahoos
Just gangs of fat women chasin' big milk shakes
If there really ain't no beer up in heaven
Then what was Saint Peter thinkin'
Or is it only the milk and the honey
We should be thinkin' bout drinkin'
Lord, Lord I hear that
Lonesome whistle blowin'

Mystery train come to carry me on back home
And when I get there
I'll sneak in a six pack in on me
Just to help me little further along
On down that celestial road.
bridge
And if there really ain't no beer up in heaven
And there's nothing up there to drink
I'd better start in right away
Think I'll drink it all today
Then on into the night, I think
Beers in heaven,
Beers up in heaven.

PRISCILLA

Livin' at the Heartbreak Hotel
Rollin like the tumblin' dice
Last time I saw you
Was like I didn't know you
You know you wasn't very nice
Feel like I'm like losing a lover
Feel like I'm losing a friend
Feel like for sure
Don't wanna see you no more
I sure don't wanna see you again
Well, I know that it's wrong but
I keep holdin' on to
A feeling that is in the past
Now you're gone
Baby tell me I'm wrong

I gotta get out of here fast.
Feel like leavin' tomorrow.
No, I feel like leavin' today.
Priscilla, Priscilla got nothing left to give you.
And you got nothing to say.

This song was recorded some time ago in John Baxter's studio in Batesville. I asked John for a Sun Studio sound for this Elvis song. My method for writing it was to string several clashes together to form a narrative. Before it became evident to me that it was about Elvis himself. I was calling it Godzilla, it became Priscilla.

FUTURE SHOCK

Harp: A
Back when this whole thing got started
It really wasn't that long ago
Mankind lived without boundaries
No wars, no walls, no ego
Then Cain went out and killed his own brother
And we started fighting one another
Instead of just helping one another
So look where we're at now
We're all a headed for the future shock
Yes, yes, yes it won't be long
The future shock
The Deluge brought the new era
And we've come a long ways since then (or have we)
So never mind all the radiation
The atom ain't such a good friend

Well E equals m c square y'all
That really didn't get us nowhere y'all
Just fire and destruction in the air y'all
Burnin' like you don't know how
We're all headed for a future shock
etc---------------
ride
Incognito incommunicado
Just a runnin' down
The road well come on
I'm the derelict hobo the lonesome dark stranger
And a long long ways from my home

Here is a song that has been around for a long time. Jim Dandy is right when he says, "You have all your lifetime to write your first album, you have eight weeks for the second one." Around the time I wrote this, I was reading Alvin Toffler's *Future Shock*. He prophesizes a world of stress and disorientation brought on by information overload. When we come down to it, this is an anti-nuke song. Soon come y'all.

NO SLOP FOR YOU

Key: A; Tempo: 30

I know I loved you too much Baby
Wasn't nothin' too good for you
Now don't look at me with your big pig eyes Darlin'
Cause I've got no slop for you
I gave you every bit of my money Baby
At first, we was so happy Baby
Then I ended up with the same old blues

So don't look at me with those big pig eyes Baby
Cause I've got no more slop for you
Gave you every bit of my money Baby
And you know I was mostly always true blue
Now don't look at me with those big pig eyes Darlin'
Now Baby we're through
Someday you'll find another
Someone who will do most anything for you
Till then don't look at me with those big pig eyes
Cause I got no more slop for you.

An old saying: "Don't look at me with those big pig eyes darlin' cause I got no slop for you."
Reminds me of a Taj Mahal song.

DRAFTED BY THE SALVATION ARMY

Key: E; Tempo: 45

turn around

I only wanted to get laid off
so I could draw some unemployment
ended up ringing this here bell
in a cold downtown Delacroix
Got no family for Christmas dinner now
No one to love and enjoy
Guess I'll go down to the Army now
And spend my day at hoi poloi.
Sed I'm down and out in wintertime.
Can't seem to find a friend
But I was drafted by the Salvation Army
Now they got to take me in

So, when you're down and out in Delacroix
And you must make amends
Go get drafted by the Salvation Army, son
Then they've got to take you in.
ride
Well, I've seen my share of hardship
Done lots of deadly sin
Thank God for the Salvation Army
Was them that took me in
If you seek some sweet redemption
And if you need a friend
Just get drafted by the Salvation Army, son
Then they got to take you in
turn around
Man from the TV said that's swell
Turkey dinner for us all
Then I'll have to go and ring this here bell
At the All-American Mall
And I'm glad to know
That someday soon
I can draw some unemployment
And I can buy a one-way ticket home
Say good bye to Delacroix
Yes, I was broke and drunk in wintertime
And it looked just like the end
I got drafted by the Salvation Army, son
It was them that took me in
So, if you're broke and drunk in Delacroix
On some lost weekend
Go get drafted by the Salvation Army, son
Then they've got to take you in.

So goodbye forever Delacroix
And on that you can depend
turn around

The outstanding thing about this song is the steel guitar styling of John Rich. Thanks so much, John.

When I left my job to be a song writer, I rang the Salvation Army bell at Christmas season. That accounts for some of the input. But further, a long-time friend found himself alone one Christmas. He went to the evening dinner at the Salvation Army. A TV crew had come to the event, and they interviewed him for the news. I sat at home and watched it on the TV. Someone asked me why this song takes place in Delacroix. Well, I like the way that name sounds.

CAN'T AFFORD TO DIE

A Capella
Well, my food stamp worker's been real mean to me
And I really don't know why
My crazy check got garnished
And I can't afford to die
Employee of the month down at the dollar store
And that's not an alibi
Saint Peter please don't call my name
Cause I can't afford to die
bridge
And when it's time for me to make amends
I swear to you I'll try
But please remember until then
That I can't afford to die.
My judgement day's a drawing near

All in the sweet why and why and why
I hope I don't get what's comin' to me
When I can't afford to die
bridge
My evening sun's a sinking low
All in the sweet by and by and by
I'll stand up tall
I'll shout out loud
That I can't afford to die

"Well, my food stamp worker's been real mean to me and I really don't know why." I was a food stamp worker as a young man. Several people were trained about food stamp eligibility. Two from the same local town, myself and "Earl." Earl was an extremely meek person, not inclined to look others in the eye. We both went to work in the Welfare Office.

When Earl got behind that desk, his entire personality changed. No kidding, he was like the Gestapo. People would leave the building in tears over how they had been cross-examined. Finally, our supervisor had to strongly discuss with Earl the proper way to proceed. That's the genesis of that line of the lyrics. Some people just can't handle a little authority.

I wanted to record a field hollerin' song. Field hollerin' was a precursor to the blues. My theory is that you can't sing the blues if you haven't spent time in the cotton field on a hot August afternoon. Field hollerin' was a way that the slaves had of communicating so the master couldn't understand them when they said bad things about him behind his back. It also was a way to signal to Jehovah that the field hand was at his end and really needed to leave the sunshine and sit under the shade tree for a while. All relevant training for blues.

INCOGNITO INCOMMUNICADO

Manchild Razor and the Razorbacz, featuring Johnathon Paape.

Front cover: Manchild Razor and the Unknown.

Back of insert: The Les Paul has great potential when the natives get restless.

Middle leaf: 12399 Hollywood Boulevard, Hollywood California. Home of Dead Monkey Records.

Back cover: The printing company had a hard time understanding that this shot was supposed to look backward. Note my crossed fingers.

Songs:

Raylene: My favorite song so far. Raylene is Harlene, a friend from high school. She was indeed a beauty queen. The last time I saw her was at a class reunion. She came in very drunk and with each article of her clothing turned inside-out. Everyone avoided her. What a shame. She died not long after that and no one could come up with the money needed to bury her. Meanwhile, we were having problems with someone stealing mail out of our mailbox. One lady was caught in the act and faced severe punishment. Her name was Raylene. These two themes structure this song. … modulation…to what?

Too Wet to Plow: Someone asked me if I had heard the song *Long Tall Glasses*. I listened to it and this idea emerged. And my friend Malcom told me about a band his friend played with called The Plowboys.

I Can't Leave You, Baby: I wrote this song with my good friend and former work mate Randall Messick. We worked together in radio in Mountain Home (KTLO). The ax man commeth. This song is a confession…

Naked and Afraid: This song was written about a TV show that's very popular around my house.

Dr. Smith and Dr. Wesson: This song reminds me of my grandfather, Pete. He rode a big Harley. I ended up with his Smith and Wesson. Also, it's a true story about two friends who wanted the same girl.

Blackie Rye: A cloudy remembrance of childhood. Blackie needed his own song. He was the man who would come down the alleyway, driving his wagon pulled by two mules. In that time, people burnt their trash in a 55-gallon drum in their back yard. When the drum would fill with ash and metal, Blackie would empty it in his wagon and haul it off.

AL-UNAN: Wrote this one with Bobby Crooze. Guess what.

It's about drinking.

How's that Working Out for You?: I try to write a Beatles song for each album.

Streets of Nashville: I wrote this after my first trip to Nashville. The music of this song came from my thoughts about Cash's *Walk the Line*.

Let's Forget That You Forgot: I heard this line on a TV show, *Portlandia*. Homage to *Loose Talkin'*.

Harelip the Pope: This song's impetus comes from a David Alan Coe record. He commented about one of his songs; "If that ain't country, it'll harelip the pope." Stand by for more pope stuff.

Laughingstock of the Cul de Sac: Here again, from a TV show; someone's stand-up routine. I live on the cul de sac in question. (Debbie co-wrote this song).

All songs written by Crooze Brothers (Baba and Coy Ray), in addition; #6 and #9: CB and Jonnie Luger; #7: CB and Johnathon Paape; #11: CB and Michael Million.

RAYLENE

Key: D; Tempo: 50

Raylene
You won't even try to talk to me
Well, when I get back
You better be
Home alone tonight
Cause baby
I think tonight just might be
The very end for you and me
if you start one more fight

verse two

Cause Raylene
If you're gone again, it could mean
That's the last time you'll ever see me
there in your bed
Between
All the hurtful things your friends say
And that awful scene you threw today
Darlin' what got in your head huh?

bridge

And Raylene
I know you even robbed the U.S. Mail
Girl you're gonna end up back in jail
Don't you ask for me to go your bail, this time
Raylene
You used to be a beauty queen
Now you're a worn out has been
You chasin' money all the time
And I've seen
You are sneaking back to town in tight jeans
Painted up like you was seventeen
When you were in your prime

ride

And Raylene
I know you're headed back to Walmart
With stolen credit cards
Girl that ain't smart
Please think it over sweetheart

modulate

Cause maybe

If we could only try to get away
And find another place to stay
Somewhere far away
From New Orleans
Then could be
We could even raise a family
Find a real home for you and me
I know that we could
Raylene

Raylene is my all-time favorite song I've written. Here is a bit of background. We had mail to go missing from our mailbox. The thief took a check we used to pay a bill and erased all handwriting. They took this cleared check to Walmart and purchased a very expensive vacuum. Debbie noticed the purchase and went to the police. It didn't take much investigation to find the security tape that filmed the transaction. The thief's name was Raylene. She had already been arrested on another charge and sat in a jail cell in another state. That's where I got the song title.

As I wrote the song, I started thinking about a friend from high school, Harlene. Over the course of the next few weeks the title became Harlene. That continued to change back and forth, until it stayed Raylene. But really the song is about Harlene. In school, Harlene won all the local beauty pageants and got straight As. I was surprised to see her at the class reunion. She was totally drunk and all her clothes were on inside-out. All her so-called friends tried their best to avoid her by hiding when she came close.

It wasn't long until I heard the report that she died. She was broke when she died, so the class had to take up a collection to bury her. I was on a Byrds jag at the time and wanted that style and sound for the song.

TOO WET TO PLOW

Tempo: 55; Key: G

I know you're looking for a cowboy
But would you settle for a plowboy
Was dark in here now I'm adjusted
You look at me you're so disgusted
I want to dance but I just don't know how
But I'm standing right here right now
And I'm so lonesome for someone some how
But I can't dance and it's too wet to plow
Won't do no one no good any how
You seem to me to be frustrated
But I know love is overrated
You look at me and you raise your eyebrow
I've never done this type of thing no how
Don't look at me like I'm way too low brow
Cause I can't dance and it's too wet to plow
Gets mighty lonesome on the home stead uh huh
Sleepin' single in a double bed
I wanted city lights instead
It's rainin' anyway so go ahead
But when I got here
The place was dead
Still, I couldn't get you out of my head
I gotta make a move but I don't know how
Cause I can't dance and it's too wet to plow
Well, I can't dance
≠I don't know what to do with my hands
And I don't know just how to stand
But I know I need some quick romance

Please just give me a second chance
So disjointed-what to do with my feet
And it's so easy to see
That Frankenstein could
Dance much better than me
I wanna be just like that guy on TV
He glides around the room so casually
And maybe I could just try in a while
To move my groove thing and give you a smile, here goes
ride
I can dance I can dance I can dance like Don Ameche
I can dance I can dance I can dance
Like Fred Astaire
I can dance I can dance I can dance like John Travolta
I can dance just like Tom Cruise in his underwear
Now watch me dance in my underwear
Here I go
ride

CAN'T LEAVE YOU BABY (IF YOU'RE ALEADY GONE)

You said you was leavin' tomorrow
That you'd break up our little home
I thought that you was so happy now
I should have known better all along
My next stop is at the Circle J bar
Gonna drink till I'm visibly stoned
Cause I can't leave you Baby
If you're already gone
These past few hours I've been wandering on

Come out of some foggy nowhere zone
Spend all my days in a forgotten haze
I start to cry
I'm on my own
Never gave you one good reason why
That you should stay on
But I can't leave you Baby
If you're already gone
Darlin in my mind
You're already gone
You're with your ma in Texas
And I'm at home alone
If anyone should ask me
You're out chasing the great unknown
Yes, I can't leave you Baby
If you're already gone
**turn around . . . ride**
I always thought that our love would last
It's written in our song
It's just the way the world should work
Two rights can't make one wrong, right?
I only wish that we could meet in dreams
And have our fates redrawn
Cause I can't leave you darling
If you're already gone
**bridge**
What a terrible thang I did that night
I pray two rights can make one wrong right
That's really all there is to say
Cause I know they'll catch me anyway
Come to sometime this mornin'

The road beneath my wheels
Don't know what road my car is on
Can't tell how my heart feels
I'll breathe a sigh and just drive on
Till I'm a thousand miles from home
I can't leave you Baby
If you're already gone
coda
RIP now Baby
Cause you're already gone

NAKED AND AFRAID

Chord Prog: Am G E; Tempo: 60; Harp: D
Naked and afraid
Just like some washed out
Some worn out renegade
With those adolescent plans you made
To carry on your transparent charade
You should have listened to me
You wouldn't be all
Naked and afraid
Naked and afraid
I tried to warn you but you stayed for 21 days
Couldn't tell you nothing
Just couldn't, ok?
When it all come down
You never been so betrayed
I really couldn't see
Why you always gotta be
Naked and afraid

So, Baby sure hope you're ready for insertion
But don't expect to hear no
drawn out sermon
**ride**
And the price you paid
For all the pleasures you
Couldn't delay
All those same mistakes you made
All God's commandments you disobeyed
Girl you lied to me
You're always gonna be
Naked and afraid
**bridge F**
And the price that you paid
For all the pleasures you couldn't delay
All of those same mistakes you made
All of God's commandments
You disobeyed
Girl, you lied to me
You're always gonna be
Naked and afraid
**bridge F**
So, Baby get ready for extraction
You're never gonna get no satisfaction
Naked and afraid
This ain't no love song no late-night serenade
Because those debts
You can never repay
Girl, you cried to me you're always gonna be
Naked and afraid
**ride and out**

DR. SMITH AND DR. WESSON

verse

Don't know for certain, sed I'm just guessin'
It's a familiar phrase, it's a slight digression
But I can tell by your surprised expression
That you respect my friends Dr. Smith and Dr. Wesson

verse

If all your inhibitions have now been overtaken
And you don't show them any bad regressions
They might just point you to a very good progression
Here's my friends Dr. Smith and Dr. Wesson

chorus

Hey, let me introduce you to my friends
Preceded only by their reputation
Start talking smack and
They might just teach you a lesson
Dr. Smith and Dr. Wesson
Dite-moi si vous avez des questions ya'll.
Cause curiosity is a mighty good weapon
It can help explain just what I'm expressin'

bridge

Don't know how I got along without them
They sure can help any negotiation
But they don't abide no provocation

ride

Hey, let me introduce you to my friends
Preceded only by their reputation
Start talking smack
They might just teach you a lesson son
Dr. Smith and Dr. Wesson

verse

So, step right in to meet up with my friends
You may find there's a mighty strong attraction
And I know you will feel
So certain about them
Dr. Smith and Dr. Wesson

Here we have the sordid story of Butch and Frank. Butch and Frank both wanted the same girl. ASU sponsored a street dance to kick off the new term. It was a big deal. The Esquires were rocking out that night. The young lady in question, we'll call J. J. was giving a lot of attention to Frank, and he was able to talk her into coming back to his house to continue the festivities. Meanwhile, Butch came to the dance looking for his girlfriend and asking about her whereabouts. He quickly found out the truth and immediately traveled the short distance to Frank's house.

When Butch commenced to pound at the door, Frank went to get his gun, a Smith and Wesson .38. He flung open the door and aimed the gun at Butch's forehead. Frank said, "Don't make me shoot you Butch." Months later, Butch and J. got married. They had a daughter. Butch never got over the gun incident. Even many years later he still talks about it whenever Frank's name is mentioned.

BLACKIE RYE

Key: B7; Tempo: 53; Harp: E

Come here Baby, you know I'll work real hard for you
I love you little Baby and I would do most anything for you
Girl I'm working 24/7

Just to make our dreams come true
I'll work overtime to do
What you want me to
And it's 24/7 Blackie Rye
harp ride
bridge
Well, I love you Baby
Like the pig loves slop
Once I start lovin'
Ain't never gonna stop
One thing Baby
Tell you for sure
That my key on the highway
Gonna open up your back door
If it's lovin' you're looking for
Then come to my house right now
I'll give you love and understanding
Even like you don't know how
When you're working twenty-four seven
Like a no-count mule to pull the plow
And I'll work overtime
Just to do what you want me to do
Now twenty-four seven Blacky Rye
ride and out

This song started as reverie on a long summer's day. I had in mind the Memphis Sound as I was listening to some Booker T. & the M.G.'s music. In my reverie, I considered a man named Blackie Rye. In the time and in the place where I lived, things were quite different from now. Each family had a fifty-five-gallon barrel placed in the alley way. They burned what would burn. Every so often, Blackie Rye would rein his two mules and wagon down the alley way and would empty all the drums of the items that wouldn't totally burn.

I have one memory that I associate with Blackie. I was six, my neighborhood compadres and I chased down the road jumping up into Blackie's wagon, then back down again. It was a time when it didn't take much to entertain us.

I felt that Blackie should have a song of his own. Now he does.

AL-UNAN

Key: A; Tempo: 47; Harp E

Come to order and call the roll.
We are united
In booze we trust
We meet here every day at happy hour
We are the Alcoholics Unanimous
We are all in good attendance
Start out with a shot of gin
Minutes are then read, our old business
My third ex-wife stalks me again
And the only twelve step program here
Is the twelve steps to the john.
And after them first fifteen beers
That should kick in real soon
So come to order, call the roll
We are united, in Trump we trust
Right here every day at happy hour
Alcoholics Unanimous

So, round after round after round we go
Hard to beat that liquid mojo
It's a tonic to the nerves they all say
Me, I can't remember any other way, except to say that
Every one's a lost soul here.

Baba Crooze

Best line: twelve steps to the john

Exceptional steel guitar by John Rich.

Too long.

Slogging through the swamp

HOW'S THAT WORKING OUT FOR YOU?

Key: Dm; Tempo: 50

You said by tomorrow I'd be sorry
Told me that this time we're truly through
You said that you're leavin' to go back to hookin'
I hope that it all works out for you
You told me you'd find somebody better
Someone you really could be true to
Somebody with prospects
Somebody with money
Now how's that working out for you?
bridge
Can't say that I would ever shame you
For wanting all those shiny things like you do
I but I guess that yes, I really do blame you
But I truly do hope that it all works out for you

bridge

And now I see you're out
Just walking the streets
You're with Jerry Mahoney
And who knows who
I hope I never see
You again Baby
But I do hope that things works out for you

A Beatles song
Lennon-like harp ride
Ride played on bridge chords
Go back to hookin' TV show *Intervention*
Wanting shiny things
Jerry Mahoney
I don't know you I meant it.

STREETS OF NASHVILLE

Key: C; Tempo: 35
I'm on my own
No place to go
But walk the streets of Nashville
From Lafayette to Music Row
I know that I will meet
A whole lot of people on the street
But none of them cares for me
I feel like I could never leave
These streets of Nashville.

And all the tourists in all the bars
Of Music City, Nashville
They all want to hear a country music star
Play all their hits in Nashville
But things just didn't pull my way
When I finally reached Broadway
I had to pawn my dad's guitar
In downtown Nashville.

I was in Denver working through pre-production of some songs. One line was: "Things just didn't go my way." But in this taping, I sang: "Things just didn't pull my way." I don't know where that came from, but I liked the way it sounded so I changed the lyrics.

LET'S FORGET THAT YOU FORGOT

So, let's forget that you forgot
About the wedding vows you once gave me
Our new home, our little baby
Forget the love I thought would save me.
So, let's forget that you forgot
About that little golden band dear
The one you wear on your sweet hand
Dear come back, forget those other men.
bridge
In this small-town world where we're livin'
There's lots of loose talking going 'round
But I don't believe it
No, not even for a minute.

I can't help but just remember
All those loving thoughts that went unspoken
And when I told you it's forever
I gave you my deepest devotion.
Why don't we just try
Once again to remember
Remember everything we both hold dear
Like the first time I held you so near
Only then we can forget that you forgot.
ride
bridge
Can't we just look on to tomorrow
Forget the strife, forget the sorrows
Let's just think about things we've got
Then we'll forget that you forgot.
Fate has granted us this one time together
Please don't throw it all away forever
Cause I still love you and I'm standing here praying
We can forget that you forgot.

This song came from a TV show I was watching, *Portlandia.* To me it sounded like a country song, that Cal Smith tune *Loose Talking*. I remember my friend, Danny Witcher, in the fourth grade. Danny stood in front of the class with guitar in hand when he sang the Smith song. He blew everyone away.

Highlights of the song are the great steel guitar work and the walking bass. Thank you, Johnny Hammer. Be sure to note there is nothing autobiographical about this song. Notice the song has a Beatles-type ending.

HAIRLIP THE POPE

Tempo: 45

You're gonna hairlip the pope
Harelip the pope
What did you smoke
What did you toke
You're gonna hairlip the pope
Gonna give him a stroke
How can he ever cope
When you harelip the pope
You left home on vacation
You come back on probation
You shocked 'em all on Duvall
When you went down in Key West
You went way 'cross the borderline
With them so-called friends of mine
I got reliable sources
Predicting nasty divorces

You gonna harelip the pope
Harelip the pope
There just ain't no hope
He's at the end of his papal robe
When you harelip the pope
Stop takin' that dope
Or you'll harelip the pope
Yeah, you'll harelip the pope.
ride x2 G7 F D
I paid all your DUIs
Girl, did I get a big surprise
You trashed my brand new mobile home

You left me here standing all alone
You even keyed my blue Camaro
Then you drove it down to de Janeiro
Robbed a bank along the way for more dinero
Wearing just an old sombrero

You're gonna harelip the pope
Harelip the pope
You walkin' on the tight rope
You're on a slippery slope
Harelip the pope
Harelip the pope
Can't see any hope
If you harelip the pope.

And now it's time to kiss the ring
But you just don't know how
Now that you've done everything
What have you done wrong now
You got to come home now
Why don't you just come home now
I'm tired and all alone
Baby, just kiss the ring
Baby, why don't you just come home now.

This song is dedicated to Milo DeSoto.

And still again a fixation on the pope. I have nothing against the pope. Just the opposite, I'm a big fan. But I know that he is just a man like all the rest of us.

This song came from several directions, including a news story and a couple of movies.

LAUGHINGSTOCK OF THE CUL DE SAC

Key: D; Tempo: 55

Now that you've gone away
Sed you wasn't comin' back
They all laugh at me
Down here on the cul de sac
You closed out our bank account
Took my Cadillac
Sed that it was payback
Laughingstock of the cul de sac
Guess I'll consult my zodiac
Read Dr. Phil's latest paperback
His advice may help my rep
Down here on the cul de sac
Now the kids just point and laugh
Cause I'm pacing like a maniac
Like a junkie that's high on crack
Laughin' stock of the cul de sac
Feelin' kinda funny
Hope it ain't no cardiac
Got the cold chills
Got the hot flash
Everything fades to black
short ride
I might just head south
Think I'll go pack
Find me a girlfriend
And an aphrodisiac
Get laid, lay back
Get my knack back with Prozac Jack

Forget they ever called me that
Laughingstock of the cul de sac
ride out

Inspired by a stand-up comedian I saw. The song mentions Dr. Phil, what a joke; he's no doctor. Got my knack back with Prozac and a prescription from Dr. Gage. Coy plays the keys.

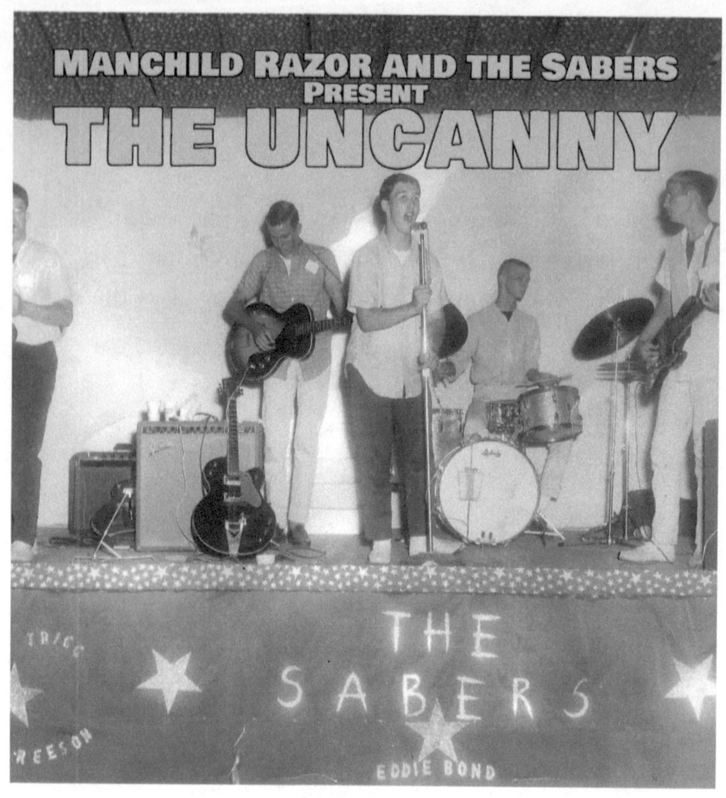

THE UNCANNY

This album is dedicated to the memories of Paul Elledge and Michael Million.

Songs

Detroit Hitman

Black Train A Comin': Key of E, Tempo 72 , two harps A over D

Snowin' in May: Tempo 56

Nashville City Jail: Key of G, Harp G, Tempo 60

Kellyanne Kellyanne: Key of E, Tempo 52

Mighty Hard Row to Hoe

The Great Hereafter

My Prayer for Me: Key of F, Tempo 37

Arky Trailer Trash: Lie, lie, lie.

The American Heart: Tempo 56

Footsies with the Nazis: Key of A, Harp D, Tempo 73

Raise the Dead (the Uncanny): Harp G over A, Tempo 66

All songs written by Manchild Razor, except:

Black Train A Comin': Razor, Michael Million, Traditional

Footsies with the Nazis: Razor and Phillip Shirley

Nashville City Jail: Razor and Debra Gage Hurd, PhD

Snowin' in May: Razor and Eddie Wiles

The American Heart: Razor and Dan Leyland

Great Hereafter: Razor and Baba Crooze

Mighty Hard Row to Hoe: Razor and Jane Hurd

All songs copyright and published by Dead Monkey Publishing Company Hollywood USA; ASCAP, Unauthorized duplication is a violation of applicable laws. All rights reserved.

Printed in USA.; Recorded in Nashville, 2021.

Thank you for the support of my friends and family, especially to Debbie.

John Sturdivant at Junction Studio made it look easy. Be sure to check out his website: JunctionStudio.com. John is a scholar and a gentleman.

John Rich does a wonderful job on the steel guitar.

Congratulations, Dr. Johnathon Paape, EdD.

DETROIT HITMAN

Key: G, modulate to A; Tempo: 54

Gonna sell my pickup truck
And hire a Detroit hitman
I'm broke. I'm down. I'm outta luck
Ain't no one can help
But maybe he can
If only things were different
I'd try to make another plan
But I'm gonna sell my pickup truck
And find a Detroit triggerman
I'm not a guy who's violent.
Got lots of love for my fellow man
I want to do the best I can
I wanna be a better man
Although I'll try to make amends
I know I'm no Superman
I'm gonna sell my pickup truck
And find a Detroit triggerman

bridge

She made a vow to stay forever
I can't believe that she wouldn't
She made a vow to love me only
I can't believe she couldn't
So, I'm gonna sell my Chevy truck
The only way for me to raise a buck
Then I'll cut out the middleman
And hire a Detroit hitman

ride

modulate to A

You gotta buy my pickup truck
Give you a deal that you can understand
I hope that you'll have lots better luck
Of holding on to your baby's hand
I only want to sell my truck to
Somebody who can comprehend
I'm gonna sell my pickup truck
And hire a Detroit hitman.

One of my notes: Johnny Rodrigues? That's what I heard in this song, Johnny Rodrigues. This is surely one of my favorites in this set. This song springs from an old saying at home, "I'm gonna sell my pickup truck and hire a Detroit hitman." Meaning, you are extremely displeasured, and you are going over your options. In the song, the young man has run out of options, and must proceed with his only perceived avenue.

"Not a man who's violent." Clearly passive/aggressive in nature.

Yada yada yada.

She made a vow to always love me. Reoccurring theme in these albums. It's on my mind.

Chevy truck. My hat off to George "try me" Nunally. We can only wish him well. Like the singer says in the song, he ran out of options.

BLACK TRAIN A COMIN'

Key: E; Tempo: 72; Harps: A and D;
Sonny Boy Williams Traditional

Black train a comin'
And I believe that I'm fixin' to die
Black train keeps right on rollin'
And I believe that I'm fixin' to die
Well, I don't mind dyin'
But I hate to see my children cry.
And then there'll be two black horses that will carry me
Tote me to the depot and eternity
There'll be two black stallions that will carry me
One name Truth and one named Perfidy
And I'm afraid to see
What this old world turns out to be 'cause
Yonder stands the hangman
Wants to lay his brand-new rope on me.
ride
And there's only one thing that I'll ever ask of you
Only one thing I want you to do
I said there's only one thing
I'll ever ask of you.
Jess see that my grave is kept clean
Bobby, see that my grave is kept clean.
ride
This ball and chain
The only thang
Left here to keep me company
Sed that the poor can't take no more
So, what will be will be

For a derelict hobo like me.
Jess lay two pennies
On my tomb stone
To pay my fare on
To the other side.
Train, train
Train arrive
Gonna ride I'm gonna ride
Black train a comin'; black train arrive
Black train a comin'; Someone must die.

This song is an all-time favorite because of its connection to Michael Million. I knew Michael from way back in the Jonesboro days. We were in a couple of music groups together, but nothing ever jelled. Michael played his own instrumentals. He would give names to these songs.

Dave and I went to see him, and he played a new tune, I asked the title. He said "*Black Train a Comin'*." I liked it. I told him I thought that sounded like the title to a delta blues song, could I use it? He said "sure." In my notes, I write: "traditional, Sonny Boy Williams, Hendrix." That's the way it sounded in my head. It turned out to be more like a New Orleans funeral march.

Once I had a transcendental experience while riding on a train. Now I see this is all linked. Please note that Debra schooled me about older times and burial rites. I do believe that this song is about my own and personal mortality. At 74, I wait for the Black Train.

Of course, the Black Train is the Mystery Train. The back story of the song involves a drifter that has been arrested and wrongly found guilty. He waits for the rope and asks his friend to see that his grave is kept clean.

Horse named "perfidy," from a Johnny Cash song.

Perfidy = untruth.

He hears the train whistle approach and his redemption draweth nigh.

SNOWIN' IN MAY

George Jones is gone and gone
He left here to stay
RIP, George Jones is gone
And now it's snowin' in May.
Say, don't the world seem just a little bit colder now
And that we're all just a little bit
Further from the sun
Cause George Jones died today
And now it's snowin' in May
We played his records on the lonesome juke box
At the Hotel Noble
All night long into the deep dank delta dawn
And we loved it when he used to try to sing like Hank
And we would all sing along
With a why baby, why baby, why baby, why
And those August nights so long
Time passes slow in the deep delta dawn
He made a million dollars by not showin' up they say
Cause he had one hundred fifty hits in a row
All his fans would still line up for tickets though
When everybody knew
He wouldn't show
Cause George was disposed to the barley corn you know
What touring star could ever just say no?

But he took it way too far though
Livin' and dyin' with the choices that he made
Tammy stood by her man they say
But He Stopped Loving Her Today
ride
It was the first day of May when we got the news
Then there came an unexpected deep snow
It never happened before though
No one could remember such a late snow here so
I thought a lot about that day
That first day of May
The late snow was like the country songs
That George played.
His classic country sound now seemed so out of time
And when the May sun come out to shine
The snow was melting away
Just like the songs that George played
Out of date and out of mind
Would soon just fade away
And like George asked us and I'll ask it too
Who, who's gonna fill those shoes?
George Jones is gone and gone
He left us here to stay
RIP, George Jones is gone
And now it's snowin' in May
Hey, don't the world turn just a little bit slower now
And we're all just a bit further from the sun, son
Cause George Jones died today
And now it's snowin' in May
vamp and out

NASHVILLE CITY JAIL

Key: G; Tempo: 60; Harp: G

I'm in the third day of a seven day stay
In the Nashville City Jail
Well, I got pulled over with some contraband
So, the cop he had to take me in
But I really don't mind so much at all
Jail's better than what's at home.
A case of mistaken identity
The guy they're chasin' looks a lot like me
But when they ran my name through ISD
Well, that was all she wrote
Now I sit on cell block three
With no one at all to go my legal bail
But if only I had angel wings to fly
I'd fly right outta this jail

bridge

And she don't care if I am gone
She would not accept my call on the telephone
When I get out of here again
I'll get on board a big jet plane
And then I'll really fly away
But I'm in the third day of a seven day stay
And it's a long way outta here

ride

And she don't care if I am gone
I'd be better off
If I was on my own
But it's better now
Than it was yesterday

More than one way out they say
But today I guess I'll stay
I'm in the third day of a seven day stay
In the Nashville City Jail

Debbie started me on this song by telling me about a Marilyn Manson lyric, something about being on the third day of a seven-day binge. In my mind, it sounded like the Eagles. Freud is key to the lyric of the song and to the entire album.

A fleckless man ends up in jail and is contemplating doing something extreme. Or should he just wait it out?

Great drumming, John.

My favorite line: It's a long way outta here.

KELLYANNE KELLYANNE

Key: E; Tempo: 52

Kellyanne Kellyanne
Please read this letter then you'll understand
I saw your picture at the news stands
You sellin' shoes out of the grandstand
Kellyanne Kellyanne
I'd love to take you to the hinterland
We'll do a motor tour of Dixieland
We can even take some contraband
But baby, gee, only if you want to.
So, tell me, Anne, Kellyanne
Will you just meet me baby at the break
Say you'll see me by the bandstand
Don't even talk about no caravan

I saw your eyes change from blue to bland
That awful April day you bombed Iran
So, I was headed to the Rio Grande
Thought I'd drop in just to hear the band play
And maybe just see
What I could get into
bridge
Just picture us in the wild, blazing nighttime
We're flying closer to the borderline
I'm holding tight onto your waist band
And then you go and do a handstand
I think I love you Kellyanne.
ride—Chuck Berry
I remember when you was Blue Berry Queen, girl
That was way back in 2016, girl
And you was working at the dollar store
Here they come Baby,
Better not say no more
Please read my letter Kellyanne.
ride and out
Kellyanne!

In my mind, this song started as a Chuck Berry song. It morphed into something else. The backstory to this song is that a young man gets a crush, a fixation on Kellyanne. He wants to contact her despite the rigid security. He writes her a letter and waits for his chance. He throws the missive over the fence as she boards her helicopter. If she would only read it, then she would understand. But no, she never notices the letter, and he is hauled off by the FBI.

MIGHTY HARD ROW TO HOE

Key: D-A; Played in three-quarter time

Hot sun poured on a delta farm
Daddy handed me a long-handled hoe
Sed, I need your help this year on the farm, son
You can't be lazy, can't be slow
You gotta know just what to chop down there
And what to leave to grow
So, the family can have a good stand of cotton
And pay off that damn bank loan.
There's shade on the other end of that row there
And cool water too at the end there
But first you gotta get busy, now
Cause you got a mighty hard row to hoe now.
And it's a mighty hard row to hoe
Gotta pay off that note we owe
Dad told me that so long ago
Life's a mighty hard way to go
He told me that and now I know
And no matter where it is I go
I can feel the heat comin' down
On a mighty hard row
I was sixteen the day that daddy died
The flu was real bad that year
Momma prayed on her knees that he'd be saved
But I guess the good Lord just couldn't hear
He kissed my hand and then pulled me down
To whisper something in my ear
You've gotta be the man now for Ma and the girls
You've gotta hard row from here

Then he said
Life's a mighty hard row to hoe
Gonna reap just as you sow
And no matter where it is you go
Someday you'll know like I know
For your sake, I wish it wasn't always so
Where I been, what my life has showed
It's a mighty hard row
A hard row
ride
We made a vow before God and man
To always have and hold
But with two babies cryin'
She changed her mind
She told me where to go
But after all I been through now Lord
Hey, what else can I do now Lord
But to grab that long-handled hoe there
Cause the family needs a good stand to grow there
It's a mighty hard row to hoe
Gotta pay off the debt we owe
Dad told me that so long ago
Life's a mighty hard road
I've been down so now I know
That no matter where it is I go
This world's a mighty hard row to hoe.
It's a mighty hard row.
ride

Here is a tune written by myself and my sister, Jane, through email. It is based on a true surreal experience Jane and I shared on the family cotton farm; 54 acres of gumbo, delta clay. It's a story of one of John's fits. I made a couple of notes to myself: "forgive yourself" and, "They didn't invent the word 'guilt' for no reason."

GREAT HEREAFTER

Key: D minor; Tempo: 56

And I've been waiting all week long now
Just to get you all alone now
And to make all my many dreams of you come true
So girl, believe me this is just between me and you
Hey what's that you say to me my darling?
No, I ain't talkin' about forever
I'm just talkin' about right now
And what I'm here after
Sed nothing about forever after
Cause that's not what I'm here after
So, if you believe in the here after
Then you'll know what I'm after here
bridge
But you fit the demographic
And you fit the mojo too
So, I don't know why I got to explain
The hereafter thing to you
To someone like you.
ride
Cause I know what I'm hereafter
I'm not so sure what you're here after
And you may be here after I am gone, long gone

And you're left standing here and all alone, all alone
With no one here to help you sing your sweet love song
About a woman who can stand by her man
Just like the juke box says she can
But maybe you misunderstand
Or maybe you really don't remember
But you fit the demographic
And you fit the mojo too
So, I don't know why I got to explain
The hereafter thing to you
You know that's true
Someone like you.

I heard the song in my head as Moody Blues.

Bobby came up with the germ of the song. It's a shtick from the TV show *Laugh-In* about the Great Hereafter. "Do you believe in the hereafter? Well then you know what I'm here after!" This singer has trouble with commitment. This is a booty call.

MY PRAYER FOR ME

Key: F; Tempo: 38

And I'll be with someone else
Those days that go so well
You'll want someone to share it with
You'll need someone to tell
But I'll be with someone else
The times that you feel blue
You'll turn to try to see me there

You'll need me there just to talk to
And I'll be with someone else
When time has made you old
When your family leaves you all alone
And friends have turned so cold. You know who you are!
And I'll be with someone else
I'll find someone new
Yeah, I'll be with someone else
Somebody, but not you
ride
Time dissolves like melting snow
And you'll try to forget
Then you'll remember and you'll know
You can't forget me yet
On no
And all the things we could have shared
But you'll be by yourself
Yeah, you'll be all alone and lonely
And I'll be with someone else.
My prayer for you is happiness
My prayer for me is for somebody else

(I'll never forget what's-her-name.)

In my mind, this song played like an Elvis song, something like *Lovin' You*. The story of the song is that she had her chance, now he is leaving. He bemoans that he's got those same ole blues when that's what love is all about. "When your family leaves you all alone and friends have turned so cold." I hate to be the cynical one, it's just a matter of time isn't it?

My second reference to melting snow.

Too bad Elvis isn't around to sing it.

My best friend is Neil Russell. The circumstances under which I met up with Neil (on two separate random occasions) are unusual. I first met Neil in 1989 when I was trying to get to the Sangster International Airport in Montego Bay, Jamacia. I was running late to catch my flight back to the U.S. I had spent a few days in Negril and had run into bad luck there. I was robbed by some hooligans on the Seven Mile Beach.

They got most of my money, and almost took my shoes too. Lucky for me, my shoes didn't fit any of them, or I would have been broke and barefoot. They had surrounded me and pulled a knife. If you have ever found yourself in that situation, you know you have no other course except to comply. I had hidden a small amount of money in my shoe, just enough for the bus fare back to MoBay.

Time was tight when the bus pulled into the stop at the "taxi park." I had no money to pay for a taxi ride to the airport. The taxis were lined up waiting for fares. I went down the line of cars explaining my situation. I had no money for the taxi; no one was willing to help me out. I got near the end of line and one of the drivers told me that he would take me to the airport if I would wait a few minutes. The man that was kind enough to help me out was Neil Russell.

He popped the trunk and told me to put in my bag, my guitar too. In a few minutes, we had assembled a contingent of riders. We left for the airport. Postscript: I made it!

A few years passed and again I found myself on the Hip Strip, walking to a good breakfast place on Gloucester. I had decided to spend some time in Negril. I was wondering how I would get there. The time of day was early morning. No tourists yet, the shop keepers were just starting to ready the shops.

I saw a lady trying to open the metal security mesh on one shop, she was having no luck. I stopped to help her out, and we had a pleasant early morning conversation, as we tugged on the screen. I told her of my plans for Negril. She said her boyfriend could take me. The next day we made an early start. Her boyfriend turned out to be the same person who helped me out, Neil. OK, it may be a bit biographic. No I did not!

ARKY TRAILER TRASH

Key: A minor; Tempo: 60

Hey, Arky trailer trash
Just what you think it is you're lookin' at
What do you think that you are doing there
Like you thought
You could find more trash here
I'm warning you now Arky trash
Don't you go look at me again like that
Like I was somehow second class here
Like I was Arky trailer trash here.
So, tell me what it is you're lookin' at
Who do you think it is you're talkin' to?
And just why are you here hanging round
Next to my back door? Huh?
If you would only mind your own bidness
Then you'd be busy like before
So, you just go back on over there
Other side of the fence, on over there
Then you can tell me just what it is
You think it is you're lookin' at.
Hey Arky trailer trash
You got your sideburns

Foo Manchu mustache
That's why you look so much like
Arky trash, Arky trailer trash.
Hey trailer trash, now
You really ought to go back to school
They got one for people just like you
Those who don't seem to think so fast
Arkies who are cognitively demure
Outsiders, never fittin' in
So out of step. And so inept
But with no secrets to defend
They called me trailer trash behind my back
The day I staggered back down to the bank
To beg the man there for a second chance
To ask him please just will you be my friend
That was the day that Dixie died again.
ride
Now the sun is rising up
So, you better get back over there
Get on back behind that plow
Go milk the pigs
And slop the cows
You best start walking out right now
And don't you never look back over here again
You Arky trash, you're Arky trailer trash.
ride and fade out

According to my notes, it should sound like *Black Magic Woman*. Or perhaps like Mudcat's *On the Road*. The song fades out at the end.

This was in my mind because of my friend, Frank Wood. His daughter, Hope, had a band in Eureka Springs called Trailer Trash. In Eureka Springs, everywhere you look, there are road signs attempting to lure all the tourists into the shops. Inevitably these highway road signs feature the stereotype of a hillbilly: big nose, long, scraggly beard, straw hat, worn out overalls, bare feet, big toes. You get the picture, and you understand the inspiration.

My friend, Dan heard this song in a pre-production media. He predicted a negative reaction on social media because of the title. But that's my point: These stereotypes are misguided and a lie. Check out the end of the song; lie, lie, lie. So as far as the stereotypes go, I tried to line each one up and call each one a lie; count them.

In the story of the song, the singer confronts the Arky at his back door. Next morning he staggers to the bank to salvage a mortgage, but no dice. Das Capital. Bottom line: I am an Arkie, and I did live in a mobile home and tried to deal with the banks. I even worked in a factory building mobile homes (till the FBI f***ed that up. That's another story.) I am Arky trailer trash.

THE AMERICAN HEART LYRICS

Tempo: 56

A young boy said to his grandpa,
Granddad, please explain this to me.
All the things that are on the TV
It's so confusing and hard to see
You know they all yell and they all swear
I hoped that you could tell me where

We are going and what will happen
When we get there
Grandad smiled and then he said
Yes, I'll explain it to you the best I can
Then one day real soon, son
You'll be a man too
You'll be explaining these things to
Someone you really love too
It's the American heart
It's the fabric of our lives
You can't bend it or tear it apart
Cause it's a one of a kind
A place where the freedom bell rings
Where Lady Liberty sings
It's the American dream
For an American heart
You can feel it down at ground zero
Near the roaring traffic hum
And in New York's concrete
Where it vibrates the street
And it vibrates the street.
And it beats just like a jungle drum.
And you see it in the faces of the first-grade class
As they stand there saluting together
And in the eyes of our vets
And where the unknown soldier lies at rest
And you see it in the Fourth of July fireworks parade.
And in the Constitution too, son
So, my advice to you, son
Go read the Bible and the Constitution.
It's the American dream.

Holding on to the blood line
Forged in fire out of U.S. steel.
Best believe that it's one of a kind.
A place where the Freedom Bell still rings.
And Lady Liberty still sings.
It's the American dream
For the American heart.

PLAYING FOOTSIES WITH THE NAZIS

Tempo: 76; Harp: A

Just playing footsie with the Nazis
And kissy, kissy with the Reds
Gracey Slick and all her Wall Street Bolsheviks
Done climbed up inside your head.
Then when Ludwick
Couldn't turn the trick
Wagner quickly left the line
They all hurried back to Moscow
Just to try to have a good time
Patty cake with the Gestapo
Such a peachy lunch with Nietzsche
Playing footsie with the Nazis
It's verboten and real creepy
ride
And you was there that fateful day
The Eastern Wall came tumbling down
Everybody come out to play
When the Eichmann come around
Chasin' Eva round the bunker

Fuhrer got to have a thrill
But when they get too close for comfort
We gotta pop them little pills
bridge
Now in every history lesson
They ask that same old question of "Who?"
"Who did it, WHO?"
"Who ate off Hitler?"
Getting social with the socialists
While they're still waiting just to choose
How can we all stay silent?
When we've got so much to lose?
Playing footsy with the Nazis, you son
Them guys can't even spell revolution
Schadenfreude.

RAISE THE DEAD

Tempo: 63
Please, please me my darlings my dears
And don't you make me have to come up them stairs
You know you're making way too much racket up there
Won't you be a little quiet tonight?
Don't make me have to come up there
And read you the riot.
Just give me a little peace and quiet tonight
And peace of mind when I come home at night
Better remember just what I said
You're making way too much noise up there
What with your Beatles and your Grateful Deads
It's enough Dead to raise the dead I said

I know a lady she once told me, she said
Better watch out, that she was so sexy
She could raise the dead.
And sure, enough later that same night just like she said
She gave eyesight to the blind.
And then she raised the dead
Raise the dead, raise the dead
That's what they all said.
Handling fire and rattle snakes too
Just like the Bible said they'd do.
But when they all start speaking in tongues
That's when I know I just don't belong.
And there's really nothing else they can do

(The Uncanny)

It's like the Kinks, but with more cowbell.

When I was writing this song, I was reading *The Uncanny*, a Freud book Debbie got me for Christmas. My notes from the time tell me "More cowbell!" In my head, it sounded like The Kinks.

Background story: The singer comes home from a hard day's work. The only thing to greet him is the record player playing upstairs at full volume when all he wants is a little peace of mind. He reminisces about a girl that could heal the sick and raise the dead. This is a New Testament inspired song. Do some research if you get the time.

One reason that I am so interested in these matters is because my mother belonged to a "Hard Shell" Baptist congregation in Mississippi. She would go to visit kin nearby and later she would take me along to church. I saw several of the rituals they practiced that I would classify as "uncanny."

The Pope of Rock 'n' Roll

Songs:

Temptations of Eve

Whiskey Diet

Outskirts of Nashville

Fourth World Man

Outta Luck

All Along the Borderline

The Pope of Rock 'n' Roll

Burnt Chile

Apocalypse Next Week

Ferryboat to Algiers

Coyboy Lament

A Song for Dixie

All songs are written by the Crooze Brothers (Baba and Coy Ray) herein known as CB.

Exceptions: #6 and #9 written by CB and Jonnie Luger

#7 by CB and Dr. Johnathon Paape

#11 by CB and Michael Million

These songs are published by Dead Monkey Publishing, Hollywood, USA.

TEMPTATIONS OF EVE

Key: A; Tempo: 74 (3/4 Time); Starts on A; Harp A/E

I look back on my life, Bobby
And I seem so naive
Just to think about those wasted days
And the big lie that I believed
False promises of this old world
And how they deceive
I'm left with
Cocaine, John Barleycorn and temptations of Eve.

turn around

Born into a Christian home
But I wanted to leave
Thought bright lights would buy me happiness
But I found no release
My poor mom and my daddy
Oh lord they did grieve
Cause of cocaine, John Barleycorn and temptations of Eve.

bridge

The heart ache, the hardship
Who could foresee
That my innocence, my ignorance
I could not retrieve
Cause they was stole away, gone in the night
Just like a thief
By cocaine, John Barleycorn and the apple of Eden

turn around

ride 8 bars

So I stand here before you

Begging reprieve
I can't blame you my brothers
If you disbelieve
So, I preach now
My dear friends
You're about to receive
Evils of
Cocaine, John Barleycorn and temptations of Eve.
turn around
out (retard)

WHISKEY DIET

Key: G; Tempo: 76

Well, I went on a whisky diet tonight
And I've already lost three days
You may think I'm wasted
But I'm back in black,
I made a comeback
Look at me, I'm back in spades
Hey, I tried and tried but even I
Can't seem to change these wicked ways
But I've been on a whiskey diet here lately
And I've already lost three days.
bridge
Or maybe I lost even four by now or
Maybe even more by now, or
I could accidentally get sober
But then, please tell me what for
If I pass out on the floor, again tonight

Don't worry, sed I'll be alright.
I tried to write a song about drinkin'
But couldn't make it past the first eight bars
I tried to write a song about love makin'
Couldn't bring it to a climax
It was much too hard, and
Though it was never my intention
See all y'all at my Christmas intervention
Jameson Pickelback helps me through it
No happy hour on Sunday
But we'll burn that bridge when we get to it
ride
And this whiskey diet is like some worn out vacation
And I don't care if it harelips the entire nation
I'm gonna start right here right now on my avocation
Just sayin' that I'm sorry
Won't make things right
So, I'll go on a whiskey diet again tonight
Whiskey is cheaper than therapy
Whiskey is cheaper.
end in E

I imagined the melody to be like the song: *Snowbird*, but with a Buck Owens twist.

Before the Plague, Debbie would on occasion go to Little Rock on business. A few times I went along. She met her coworkers near the River Market area adjacent to the Arkansas River. The area was dilapidated not so long ago but is now a jewel that was rescued by the city, using federal funds. Rick Redden and his AMR Architects designed a very interesting section of the city, terminating at the Clinton Library. I knew

Rick Redden and had several successful projects with him on the UA campus. There are lots of bars and good places to eat at the River Market (but not much veggie).

When Debbie finished her meetings, we would start bar hopping. One good place is the bar Big Whiskey; me drinking whiskey on the rocks, and Debbie drinking margaritas. The barkeep wore a black t-shirt with white lettering; "I went on a whiskey diet, and I've already lost three days." Bingo!

OUTSKIRTS OF NASHVILLE

Key: D; Tempo: 88

And gold is where you find it
On the outskirts of Nashville
See the motels and the neon signs, oh how they shine
They all point you there towards the outskirts of Nashville
So, let me tell you why I say this is the end
And I'll never come back this way again.
White line leads straight to the city line there
Here on the outskirts of Nashville
And because of what really happened here
The time we tried to buy a thrill
The highway seems to have no bend
The hitchhiker, he seems to have no friend
Headed on down to Nashville again.
And the lonesome road is without an end
And no way for us to try to ever make amends
To God and to our mothers dear
Each one shines like the other does here
On account of the RV, we parked that night
We can never go back to the simple life

No not again
Not on the outskirts of Nashville
Oh no!
ride
Yea, and I've never seen that scene since then
Not since I got back to Nashville again
To the endless Broadway porn stars and the fried chicken shacks
And the pawn shops filled up with dusty Gibson ax
But it really wasn't all that it appeared to be to me
All this fuss about parking one RV
Now I'm the one they wait to kill
On the outskirts of Nashville
slide

(Confessions of the Hammer Man)

FOURTH WORLD MAN

Key: A sharp; Tempo 60
First World man sez
I'll take what's mine
I'll take what's yours too
Cause I don't care about you
Second world man sez
What can I buy now
Don't worry about tomorrow
And their pathetic sorrow
The third world man
Keeps doing all he can

He says let's all just try to get along together
Don't need nothing from you
Me or my brothers too
Take what you want
Go back where you belong
But the fourth world man
He does about all he can
To make the world a better place
To live in
It all just seems to me
Things aren't what they seem to be
But how can we abandon
Such a friend
And the fourth world man
He really cannot understand
That no matter the cost that there is to pay
We really gotta give it away
Gotta do it someday
Why not give it all away
Give it all away today
And at the stroke of midnight
There came a loud shout
Behold, the bridegroom commeth y'all
While the bride's maids trimmed their wicks
They ran out of oil real quick
And didn't make it to the party after all

OUTTA LUCK

Key: G; Tempo: 52

I'm outta tune
I'm outta time
I'm outta money
That ain't so funny
Outta resistance
Almost outta patience cause
I'm outta luck
I'm outta booze
I'm outta weed
Don't need no shoes
Ain't got no feet
Outta my mind
I'm outta here cause
I'm outta luck
So, I went to talk to my brother
Brother can you spare me a little cash, huh?
Ed said, "one brother to another,
You know you're talking way too much smack, Jack."
Outta compassion
Got no way home
Ain't got no phone
I'm outta here
I'm outta compliance
Fresh outta sympathy cause
I'm outta luck
Yes I am
ride
Yes wellum, wellum mam
I'm outta luck.

In memory of my brother, Ed.

I was never very close to my father, John. He was always working, trying to make some money and pay some bills, what with three children. I've got to say that my attitude was usually not so good toward him. We just couldn't seem to get along together. It just seemed that we both spoke different languages. One hope I had for this book and these songs was that I would be able to pull up to the surface of my subconscious mind material that I could use in a song.

It worked. As I considered the words and intent of the song, I started to remember an occurrence from a time I was in junior high. One day I stood in the shower after a day under the sun.

I was hungry and anticipating one of my mother's wonderful dinners. She stood in the hall outside the bathroom and told me that dinner was on the table. I asked her "What?" meaning what would we be eating. Then suddenly the shower curtain jerked open. There stood my father, John, red-faced, in a rage. He thought that my asking what we were having to eat was disrespectful.

He told me, "Say wellum!" With that he backhanded me. Hard. His ring stung my face. I was trying to decipher what he had just said. He slapped me again, but this time harder, still. "SAY WELLUM!" I meekly mumbled "wellum," trying not to cry. He seemed to be satisfied. He turned and left me there, standing in the shower and wondering what to do. I went to my bedroom, laid down and tried to make sense about what had just happened.

This is an example of what I predicted: songwriting can be a tool with which we may perhaps dredge up psychic materials to use in songwriting and in self-psychotherapy. Things just didn't pull my way (less dramatic, equally illustrative).

ALL ALONG THE BORDERLINE

Why can't we all just get along
Why make your brothers stay away
I came across a wall out there
Way out in Mohave today
It was a wall that stands so tall
And it gleams in the sunsplash afternoon
From Brownsville on up to Nogales
But I think the wall will fall real soon
So, all along the borderline
That's where we cast our pearl at swine
And hang out there beside the baseline
Killin' time with a girl of mine
Both of us thinking about another sin
No way for us to ever make amends
So was the wall built to keep us out
Or to keep mother nature in
And down in Mexico
We got a say
That we live on the happy side
When you insist that we all stay away
What does that make your side then y'all
Cause it's a fake wall after all
It appears much wider than it is tall
And just like all bogus walls
It eventually will fall
See it in the news
Falling down after all
ride

We need more bridges, not more walls
Then someday we can all stay
All along the borderline
On down Mexicali way
And for all of those who say to me
We must be prisoners to be free
That wall will fall down on you and on me
And on all of us, all
Along the borderline.

THE POPE OF ROCK N' ROLL

Key: G7; Tempo: 94
Hey, don't touch me I'm the pope
The pope of rock and roll
Ayatollah of rock 'n' rolla
So, don't touch me
I'm the pope
Khomeini of R & B
And any other blues that you might choose
Sed I'm the new pontiff
Just got into town
Don't wanna see nobody
Doggin' around
bridge
And don't you even try
To look at me directly in the eye
Cause if you do
I'm comin' right on after you
Yea I'm the pope

That just what popes do
The hoi polloi
They wanna walk up and grope
But then I've just gotta tell 'em nope
I won't do it
Cause I'm the pope
Said I'm the pope of rock 'n' roll
I'm the czar of things bizarre
Depository of R & B
So don't forget that I'm the pope
Whenever I hit the dance floor, see
And here I go (*3rd chord all skate*)
ride
bridge
Yea, it's easy money, baby
Just like I hoped
Mujahideen of the American dream
People might ask me just about anything
But no, don't you touch my golden suit no more
Cause if you do,
I'll excommunicate you
Well, I used to work in the grocery store
But I got news for you baby
I don't work there no more
Cause I'm the pope
I said I'm the pope of rock 'n' roll
I'm the last hope of rock 'n' roll.

BURNT CHILE

Key: A; Tempo: 52; Harp: A -- D in-hole on three

You've got to pity the fool
The lonely heart that climbs the stair
Up to an empty room
To find that she's no longer there
He pours out his heart
He falls down on his knees
He prays and he pleads
Just to have some mercy please
Pity the fool
Believes just what he hears
Bout a love and a happiness
To last through the years
Yes, pity the fool that thinks that day will ever come
When she'll need him at home as much as he needs her alone
You damn right he's got the blues
Got nothing left to lose
He's like a burnt chile afraid
Burnt chile afraid of the fire
ride
Once loved you baby, but not no more, no
All my friends they tried so hard to warn me
But I was the very last one to know,
I reached out to you my darling
My heart was there in my hand
I reached out to touch you baby
I got burned real bad
And damn right now I got the blues
I'm burnin' a fast fuse

So, I'm like the burnt chile
Burnt chile afraid of your fire.
ride
Sed I'm so broke up y'all
Cause there's another mule
Been kickin in my stall
End on a Oh Law!

This song reminds me of Bobby "Blue" Bland from Memphis, Tennessee. And finally I have that psychic breakthrough I predicted. Thinking about this song triggered in me two almost forgotten occurrences that brought about castigation in me at the time.

APOCALYPSE NEXT WEEK

Key: E; Tempo 100
Friends please don't let your knees go weak
I really don't wanna tell you this at all, no
But it's been going around the cul de sac all week
That the apocalypse is coming real soon, son
Should be here one day next week
Yea apocalypse is coming soon
Apocalypse next week.
And it's coming to a town somewhere near you
So, traverse the abyss
And then just bid adieu
As much as you can do when you're without a clue
So just for you
Here's a special witch's brew

Please, please Mr. Zombie
I knew you'd be comin' someday soon
To kick my A over the dark side of the moon
Just like the catty in that there cartoon
Guess I didn't even notice the spooky moon
But I never thought you'd be here, so soon
All on this dog day afternoon
bridge
Hey zombie woman, you know I really love your gypsy eyes
Won't you ta ta ta tell your zombie man
I don't really wanna be a zombie
Don't comprehend I can
Hey zombie woman
Darlin' won't you
Tell that zombie man
That please Mr. Zombie don't wanna go right now, no
Cause I'm not really ready as I might appear to you two
Never had a late night with Marilyn Monroe
Or my day at the park with Joe DiMaggio
Guess I should have watched lots more of them episodes
Then I could have learned more means more ways to go
To take them mean ole walkers down.
Then head down south
And slide on outta town.
Hey zombie woman
Wanta meet me later for a drink, huh
Then we could talk better
Me and you I think, uh huh
You know I really do
just need a girl I can talk to

Someone to just pray for me
When we'll feed the rich to the hungry
There's room for all of us
Here on this land
Zombie woman
Girl, take me by the hand.

(conversation at a yard sale)

FERRYBOAT TO ALGIERS

Key: D; Tempo: 69
Cast my memory back there, Lord
Over miles and through the years
Then my thoughts keeps on returning
To the ferryboat to Algiers
Like that day when I first saw you
In my reverie you appear
Stepping on down from Canal Street
Onto the ferryboat to Algiers
It was stormy on that ferryboat ride
You swooned. I held you near
You swooned and then I swept you away
Or down to Vieux Carré
Girl, do you remember?
ride
Take me back now, lord to younger days
Back to a time I held her near
When she sighed a sigh and she kissed me sweetly
On that ferry boat to Algiers.

And my life's a veil of years
But I always remember you, my love
And that ferryboat to Algiers
While we ride away on wings of memory
On that ferryboat ride towards Algiers
So, let the ferryboat fly away
On down to Algiers.
ride

I imagined a bossa nova beat, sounding like Buffett. I wanted to add claves to the mix.

This song is a love song, from me to Debbie. It is a song that wrote itself over a period of time. It is based on a real experience in New Orleans on the ferry boat that runs from the end of Canal Street. It crosses the Mississippi River and docks in Algiers, hence the Canal Street Ferryboat. I had heard about it before, but for some reason, thought it was miles away in the opposite direction. In reality it is very close to the French Quarter, about a twenty-minute walk to the north you will see the large ferry boat. Algiers is where most of the Mardi Gras accoutrement is stored till the next year rolls around. The prominent feature of Algiers is that area where rows of warehouses sit. It is where this Fat Tuesday treasure is stored. And to the north is the small village of Algiers. The quaint village reminds me of Eureka Springs, Arkansas.

Debbie and I got on the ferry and had a good time exploring Algiers. We were headed back to catch the ferry back to Canal Street. The ferryboat docked and we got on board. The water had gotten very choppy, the humidity severe. As we started out into the Mississippi, Debbie seemed to wilt from the strong motions of the boat and the heat of the sun. She swooned. A helpful man nearby pointed out an area of the boat that was air conditioned. Debbie felt much better there, and by the time we reached Canal Street she seemed fine.

Debbie adds this: "We had been drinking at the World Trade Center, way up high where you can see the Mississippi River in all its mystery and glory. We probably had more than enough to drink, but we were holding our own as we walked to the ferry boat. As a general rule, I am troubled by a combination of alcohol, heat, and motion. As I was riding the ferry boat, and looking out onto the river, I knew something was about to happen. That something was heralded by a sudden feeling that a sheet of yellow gauze was pouring over me. Or that I was melting. Either way it wasn't good. In fact, I was very close to passing out. A kind gentleman was smart enough to see my dilemma and ushered me into an air-conditioned spot where I recovered. Passing out on a ferry boat to Algiers was not what I had in mind after the second margarita. Maybe on the third, but not the second."

I hope these lyrics will speak for themselves.

COYBOY LAMENT

Key: C; Tempo: 80

Making his way
Up the old Chisholm Trail
On his very last cattle drive
Almost to McGerty
He's all worn out and thirsty
But you know that the wolf will survive
Amarillo to Kansas City
By way of Tonapaw

It's the end of an era
For all the things he knows
Things will never be
Like they was before
Then sitting by the campfire that night
Just thinking and drinking his joe
A pale rider does approach the campfire light
It's his best friend from back home
Be careful when you get back to Amarillo son
Cause he claims he'll bushwhack you there
So, Cowboy wrote a short missive
He sealed it and he kissed it
And handed it there to his friend
Please take this note to her
Tell her that I love her
I want to see her, she knows where and when
But when Cowboy got back to Amarillo
She was gone like she said she'd do
Took his reason to live
Took his heart too
So he reined his horse into the Texas sunset
Went looking for another trail ride
Heading north on the old Chisholm Trail
But never to arrive.

This song is about the last cattle dive north on the old Chisholm Trail. It was influenced by Michael Million and Frank Wood. One thing we all had in common was a love of making music. Michael wrote lots of songs, and all of them were instrumentals as far as I know, no lyrics. Each of Mike's songs had an interesting title. One of his songs was *Cowboy Lament*. I can't remember the melody he played, but I did remember the title. "Cowboy Lament" is close to *Cowboy's Lament* a.k.a. *Streets of Laredo*. To me, *Cowboy Lament* is like that western tune with the similar title. I would guess that that song would be over 200 years old and not copyrightable. Hats off to Frank and Michael for their wonderful songs and good nature.

A SONG FOR DIXIE

Key: B7 to E; Tempo: 63; Harp: C

So, let's all sing a song
A song for Dixie
So, raise your heart
And raise your glass
Let's all sing this song at last
Gonna sing it at last
And when the book of life be read
And the final roll be called
Then please let it be said
That I was proud
Proud most of all
Proud to be a son of Dixie
She was mistreated
And has now much strife back when
But now her future looks so bright ahead again
And the sun is shining bright once again
For my Dixie
So, here's to Johnny
To Uncle Ronnie

And here's to Levon too
Here's to all of Dixie's daughters and sons
That sang their sad song for you
And when my days on Earth are finally through
I'll still sing one more song
And my song is a song for Dixie
And yea, I'll sing this Dixie song
So, all y'all can sing it along
Now let's all sing this Dixie song.
refrain

I am an Arky and have lived in a mobile home. I think that background gives me a perspective on this topic, I must say that I do believe that Dixie has been put-upon in the past. I started thinking about songs for Dixie. I can only think of one, the one about "look away Dixieland." I believe we need a new song for Dixie.

When Pope of Rock 'N' Roll had been written, the next step was pre-production, I have some good friends in Denver, they have a recording studio. TJ helps me record what I have written for evaluation. This gives a good indication of how the songs sound in the studio, not just in my head. Also, the important work of sequencing can begin.

Several of TJ's friends drop in and watch the studio's goings on. As we listened back to my effort on *Song for Dixie*. One of TJ's friends (from South Dakota) asked TJ, "Who is this Dixie anyway?" TJ replied to her, "I've got no idea." He turned to me and asked: "Who is Dixie anyway?" I had to laugh and told him, "Dixie is not a person; Dixie is a geographical area."

OBITUARY COY HURD, PhD

Dr. Coy Hurd was born on Thanksgiving Day, Nov. 27, 1947. He left the planet Monday, March 25, 2024, at the age of 76. Fred Coy Hurd was the last-born child of John Coy Hurd and Ethel Campbell Hurd of Trumann.

He wore many hats, from university professor to radio announcer. He taught research, statistics and organizational management at six major universities. Dr. Hurd successfully coordinated many large capital-building projects for both the University of Arkansas and the City of Fayetteville. He retired from the University of Arkansas for Medical Sciences in 2013, where he was director of campus operations. He also was employed by the state of Arkansas and the state of Missouri. His educational career began as a graduate of Trumann High School in 1965, and he later received a bachelor's degree in sociology from Arkansas State University (1970). He completed a Master of Public Administration degree at the University of Arkansas in 1991.

He and his wife, Debra, both received the Hugh T. Henry Memorial Public Administration Award in 1990, the first time a husband and wife both won the award the same year. He was awarded a PhD from the University of Arkansas in 2000.

At one time Coy was a certified psychotherapist and a member of the American Association of Psychotherapy. He had also been a guest speaker at the Fulbright School of Public Affairs.

Coy was an accomplished musician, playing the bass guitar and keyboards, as well as writing, producing, singing and recording five well-received record albums.

As the bass guitar player for numerous bands, the awards

began stacking up, including Best Blues Band (2002, 2005, 2006, 2007) and the NWA Hall of Fame Award (2008). He opened for big musical acts such as Taj Mahal, Air Supply and Buddy Jewell. He also wrote a book detailing his life and times as a musician, and in particular, the vibrant music scenes of Northeast and Northwest Arkansas.

Coy is survived by his wife of 37 years, Dr. Debra Gage Hurd. He is also survived by a sister, Jane Hurd of Claremont, Calif.; a son, Dylan Hurd; daughter-in-law, Suki; and two grandchildren, Kaid and Jae Hurd, all of Fayetteville. He also leaves behind one great-grandchild, Penelope Hurd; a niece, Makayla Gage; and sister-in-law, Shannon Gage.

He was preceded in death by his parents and one brother, Edwin Hurd.

Coy lived most of his adult life in Fayetteville and always appreciated the opportunities that the community provided to him and his loved ones. Interment of ashes will be in Moore Cemetery at Cabanal (Carroll County) at 1 p.m. April 21.

In memory of Coy, please consider donating to the Ozark Blues Society, P.O. Box 2004, Bentonville 72712, or Paws & Claws Pet Shelter, 2075 Madison 6555, Huntsville 72740.

www.ingramcontent.com/pod-product-compliance
Lightning Source LLC
La Vergne TN
LVHW102130110826
845155LV00054B/5

* 9 7 9 8 2 1 8 5 7 2 7 9 2 *